Contents

Left: one of the gracefully curving sand dunes in the vast Sahara. The dune areas of the Sahara are called *ergs,* and make up a third of the area of the desert. The dunes are formed by the desert winds. They can move across the surface of the desert as the wind blows sand away from one side, and adds it to the other.

Frontispiece: a water color painting of a sandstorm by Lady Anne Blunt, who explored the central part of Arabia with her husband in the late 1800's. Phenomena such as sandstorms, added to the harsh climate of the desert, made exploration there particularly difficult.

List of Maps

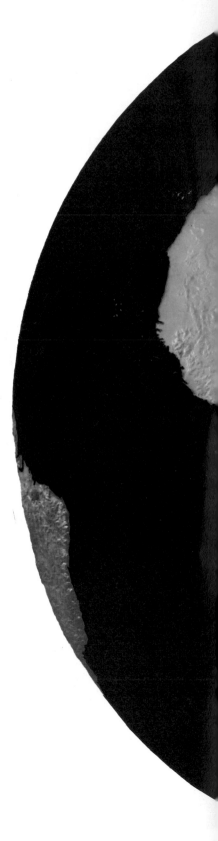

The globe, highlighting in blue the
areas where the exploration described
in this book took place. The harsh
climate and difficult terrain of these
barren desert regions, combined with
the hostility and religious fanaticism
of the desert tribesmen, made exploration in these areas particularly
hazardous. Only in the present century have European explorers finally
succeeded in conquering the deserts.

SEAS OF SAND

BY PAUL HAMILTON

Executive Coordinators: Beppie Harrison
John Mason
Design Director: Guenther Radtke
Editorial: Lee Bennett
Gail Roberts
Damian Grint
Picture Editor: Peter Cook
Research: Patricia Quick
Cartography by Geographical Projects

This edition specially produced in 1973
for International Learning Systems
Corporation Limited, London
by Aldus Books Limited, London.

© 1971 Aldus Books Limited, London.

Printed and bound in Yugoslavia by
Mladinska Knjiga, Ljubljana

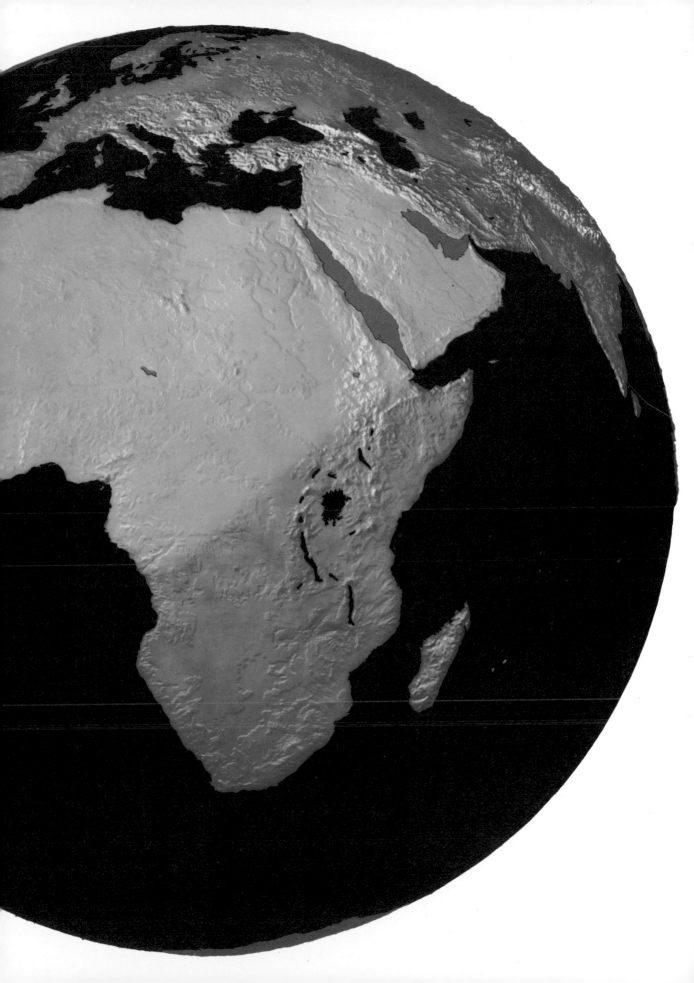

Arabia

1

Nearly a fifth of the earth's land surface is made up of desert. This does not mean that it is covered by mile after mile of sand. But it does mean that a fifth of the land is dry and barren. Some deserts are, indeed, sandy wastes. But others may be gravelly plains or rocky, mountainous areas. Deserts are not always hot either. Some are burning hot in summer and freezing cold in winter. And the wastes of Siberia and the frozen Arctic regions of Europe and North America are often referred to as *cold deserts*.

The one characteristic of all desert regions is the lack of water. In the cold deserts, all the water is frozen. In the tropical regions, rain seldom falls. When it does, it comes in short torrential down-

pours which quickly sink through the surface to the water deposits beneath. These underground water supplies feed the *oases*—the desert springs where trees and plants grow, and where the thirsty traveler can replenish his water supply. But these "islands" in the desert may be hundreds of miles apart, with nothing between but empty waste.

Few plants are native to the desert, and few animals live there. What life there is has adapted itself to the hostile environment. The camel can go for days without water. Smaller animals burrow underground to escape the heat of the sun. Desert plants can store water for long periods and lose little through evaporation. The

Above: Arabia, from Ptolemy's *Geography*. In this work, Ptolemy, a scholar from Alexandria, Egypt, summed up what was known about the world's geography in the A.D. 100's. His theories were accepted by the European world for centuries. This map dates from some 1300 years later than the original *Geography*—it was made in about 1460.

animals and plants of the Arctic regions have similarly adapted themselves to their icy homeland.

The greatest desert area in the world stretches in a broad swath across northern Africa from the Atlantic coast to the Red Sea, on into Arabia and, beyond the Persian Gulf, into Iran and Afghanistan. It reaches from the Sahara, in Africa, through the An Nafūd and Rub' al Khali deserts in Arabia and the Dasht-i-Lut and the Dasht-i-Kavir deserts in Iran, to the Dasht-i-Mārgo and the Registan deserts in Afghanistan. In Africa, the Sahara cuts off the Arab nations along the coast of the Mediterranean Sea from the Negro countries of central Africa, and is broken only by the fertile lands of the Nile Valley and a few scattered oases. The Arabian Peninsula, apart from a narrow coastal strip, is nearly all barren. For centuries, these desert lands presented an almost unanswerable challenge to travelers. The harsh climate, the lack of water, and the fierce and often fanatical tribesmen combined to make the deserts some of the most impenetrable regions of the world. Yet, despite the huge difficulties, travelers did venture into these fearsome, desolate lands. And it was to the Arabian Peninsula that they turned first.

When the first European explorers reached Arabia, there were no clear-cut political divisions because most of the peninsula was under Turkish rule. They found, however, a number of sharply defined and widely contrasting geographical regions. The Hejaz, the coastal region along the Red Sea including the holy cities of Mecca and Medina, consists of a narrow, infertile coastal plain and, inland, a high mountain range. In the south of the peninsula, in what is now Yemen, lies the Wadi Hadhramaut, a long fertile valley some 300 miles long, with walls often as much as 1,000 feet high in places. The Nejd, in the center of the peninsula, is a relatively fertile region, with towns and settlements, wadis and oases. The largest part of Arabia is, however, true desert. The rolling sand dunes of the An Nufūd and the Rub' al Khali—the Empty Quarter—stretch for mile upon mile. These arid wastes presented an irresistible challenge to European explorers.

Left: an Arabian pottery camel, from the Roman era. Models like this have been found in both the Sahara and the Arabian deserts, along the age-old caravan routes that cross the wastes.

To the early explorer, jogging along on the back of a camel at a monotonous few miles an hour, the Arabian Desert seemed like hell itself. On all sides, the sands stretch away to the distant horizon. Day after day the sun blazes down from a cloudless sky. In the three-month summer, the heat is intense, with the temperature rising in some places to 130°F, but in winter the temperature can drop to freezing point (32°F). What winds there are bring no refreshing air, but are made red hot by the sands over which they have come. All around is emptiness and silence, broken only by the sound of camels' feet plodding through the soft sand. Nor can the thirsty traveler be sure of finding water. When he reaches the scattered water holes, he may well find that they are dried up or foul.

Until the advent of the tracked automobile, the only way to cross the desert was on the back of a camel. Without the camel, life in

Above: camels in Arabia. These odd-looking animals are superbly adapted for life in the desert, and provide their masters with transportation, food, clothing, and a visible measure of their wealth and social standing. For centuries, camel caravans using traditional routes were the only way for men and goods to cross the deserts.

the desert would have been impossible for the wandering desert tribes of Arabia—it provides transportation, food, drink, and clothing. Its large soft feet enable it to travel over the sand with 200 pounds of baggage on each side of its saddle. Fully loaded, a camel can cover some 25 miles a day, but without packs it can go much farther—sometimes up to 100 miles in a single day.

The camel is remarkably well adapted in other ways to life in the desert. It can go for as much as five days without water, although the nomads do try to give their camels water to drink every day. Camels get some moisture from their food, and they retain most of the water they drink, because they sweat very little. Besides, they can eat even the driest and most prickly brushwood. And, if there is no food at all available, the camel can live on the fat stored in the hump on its back. As it uses up the fat, the hump will shrink, but as soon as it is fed properly again, the hump returns to its normal size.

As a means of travel, however, camels have their limitations. They are obstinate and bad-tempered, and will never obey commands willingly. Their unusual gait produces a strange swaying motion, which can make the traveler feel "seasick"—a fact which could have earned the camel the name "ship of the desert."

Despite the harsh desert climate, and the difficulties of travel, it is possible that the early explorers found the hostility of the nomads the greatest obstacle to their journeys. These nomads were Bedouins, a desert people who today live in much the same way as their ancient forebears. Bedouin society is divided into several classes, and throughout the class structure it is the camel that separates the superior tribesmen from the inferior. At the bottom of the Bedouin social scale are the people who live in permanent houses of mud or stone. The desert nomads despise them as being

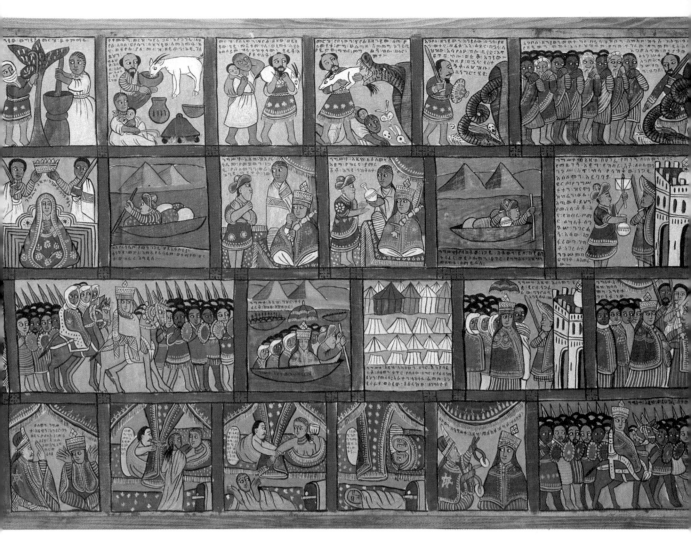

Above: more than one land has claimed the Queen of Sheba for its own. Here is an Ethiopian portrayal of their tradition of the queen, believed to have been the ancestress of their own royal line. The last two rows show the queen's visit to King Solomon.

Left: the entrance hall of the Temple of the Moon God at Marib in Yemen. In Yemenite folklore this was the palace of the Queen of Sheba. The Bible reports that she came to Solomon "with a . . . great train, with camels that bore spices and . . . gold and precious stone."

merchants of the land, and not true men of the desert. Then come the seminomads, the Aradbar tribes, who live part of the year in towns and are therefore considered to be soft by the men of the desert. The shepherds, who look after sheep and goats, are also considered inferior because sheep cannot travel as far as camels.

The aristocrats of the desert are the tribes who live in black tents made of goat's hair and sheep's wool, and spend nine months of the year—including the cooler winter months—in the heart of the desert. They raise only camels as livestock, and depend on them for all the necessities of their life. It is logical, therefore, that the Bedouins reckon their wealth by the number of camels they own.

To their natural dislike of the European intruders, the Bedouin tribesmen added extreme religious fanaticism. Their religion was Islam, and they regarded the Christian travelers as *infidels* (unbelievers) to be converted or destroyed.

The Islamic religion was founded in Arabia in the early 600's. At that time, Arabia was a primitive land where the various tribes warred constantly among themselves in an endless succession of blood feuds or intertribal quarrels. Throughout Arab society, a state of lawlessness prevailed. The Arabs worshiped idols, and the code that governed their behavior was a primitive one. Among the people of Mecca, poverty and suffering were rife. The position of women was intolerable—Arab men could marry as many wives as they chose, and divorce was commonplace. Unwanted baby girls were killed. This state of affairs would probably have continued for hundreds of years had it not been for the birth in Mecca in about 570 of one of the most remarkable men the world has ever known. That man was Mohammed.

At first, Mohammed's life was little different from that of other Arabians of his time. Then, when he was about 40 years old, he saw a vision of the angel Gabriel. Gabriel called on Mohammed to become a prophet, and to preach God's word among his fellow countrymen. This first vision was followed by others. To begin with, Mohammed told only his family and a few friends what he had seen. Then he began to preach to the people of Mecca, attacking Arab society of the time. He taught that there was only one God (Allah), and that he, Mohammed, was God's prophet. Many who heard him scoffed at his words. Others listened, and began to follow his teachings.

Mohammed's attacks on Arabian society aroused the hatred of the people of Mecca. In 622, he was forced to flee the city. His flight to Medina is called the *Hegira,* and it is from the year of the Hegira that the Moslem calendar dates. In Medina, Mohammed was welcomed as a prophet, and soon most of the people there followed his teachings. Secure, and at the head of an established religious community, Mohammed could now turn his teaching into law. He abolished idol worship, and the killing of baby girls. He limited polygamy so that Moslem men could marry no more than four wives, and he restricted the practice of divorce. Gambling and drinking intoxicating liquors were also prohibited. But perhaps Mohammed's most important reform was a ban on violence and war—except in self-defense and for the Islamic cause. This latter exception—"for the Islamic cause"—was to have far-reaching effects through the ages, and was responsible for the difficulties of many of the early explorers.

By the time Mohammed died in 632, he had been accepted as the Prophet of God by the Meccans as well as the Medinans. He was succeeded by one of his disciples, Abu Bakr, who became the first *caliph* (leader) of the Moslems. Not content merely to protect the Moslem faith in Arabia, Abu Bakr organized a *jihad* (holy war) to conquer the infidels and establish Islam throughout the world. His plans came very near to succeeding. Within a hundred years, the Islamic Empire was more widespread than that of Rome. It reached to the Pyrenees Mountains in northern Spain, throughout Arabia and Syria into present-day Afghanistan and India, and right across northern Africa. Later, it spread down into the Negro lands of east and central Africa. The Moslem invaders did afford a degree of

Below: northern Africa and the Arabian Peninsula, showing the main geographical features. For centuries, these desert regions offered little more than an exciting challenge to explorers. Today, however, vast resources of oil and minerals have been discovered under the sand, and this new wealth is bringing prosperity to the desert lands.

religious tolerance to the people they conquered, but all non-Moslems had to pay a special tax to gain exemption from army service. And, as time passed, Islam became the main religion in the conquered lands.

But in Arabia, the birthplace of Islam, religious tolerance was limited. Moslem law barred non-Moslems from entering the holy cities of Mecca and Medina on pain of death, and Christians traveling anywhere in the Arabian Peninsula did so at great risk. Yet despite the dangers which awaited them in Arabia, explorers were still

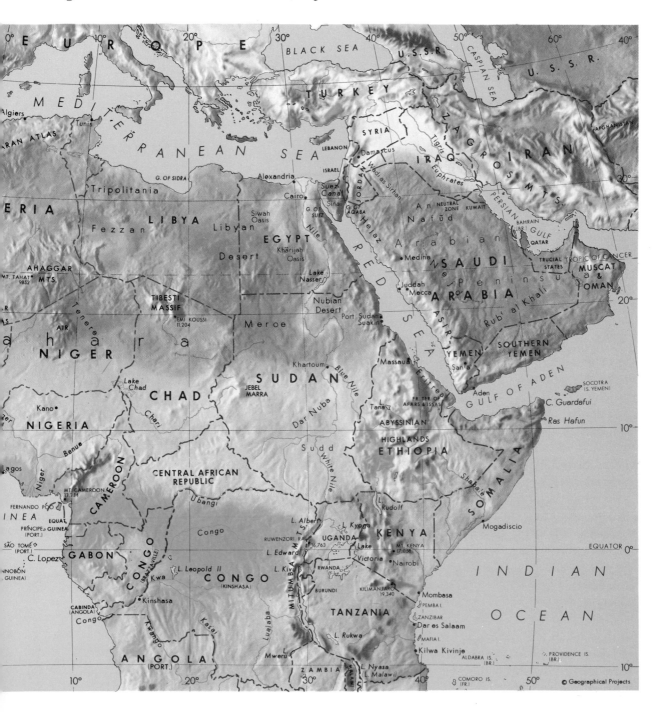

Left: a Turkish miniature of the 1500's. It shows the black tent of the aristocratic Bedouins, and a well—both sights as familiar in the desert world now as when it was painted.

willing to risk their lives to penetrate the unknown interior of the peninsula. What was it that drove them on?

First, to the natural attraction of the unknown was added the even greater lure of the forbidden—the excitement of doing something that was not permitted, at no matter what risk. So great was this lure that a few European adventurers even disguised themselves as Moslems and took part in the pilgrimage to Mecca—the *hajj*, which all Moslems must make at least once in their lives. These adventurers took part even though, had they been discovered, they would probably have been killed. The second great reason for the European interest in Arabia lay in the rumors of wealth which, for thousands of years, had circulated in Europe. The people of Yemen claim that the fabulously wealthy Queen of Sheba was their ruler, and believe that the Temple of the Moon God at Marib was her palace. Certainly, caravans used to pass through Arabia, carrying such treasures as frankincense, myrrh, cinnamon, gold, pearls, and precious stones. The legends of riches aroused the interest of European explorers and merchants alike, who determined to discover whether or not they were true.

But when the first European explorers reached Arabia, they saw little sign of this fabled wealth. The difficulties of travel were, however, ever present. And the character of the peninsula changed little as the centuries passed. A hot, dry, inhospitable land of extreme temperatures, it was inhabited by men whose hostility to travelers who did not share their faith was often fierce. It is not surprising, therefore, that it took until the 1930's for European explorers to fit together the last few pieces of the Arabian jigsaw.

Below: Arabia, showing the principal routes of the trade caravans, together with those followed by pilgrims to the holy cities of Mecca and Medina. These routes existed long before there were proper maps and, for much of their length, led through empty desert. The camel caravans, however, managed to follow the same route year after year in their journeys across Arabia.

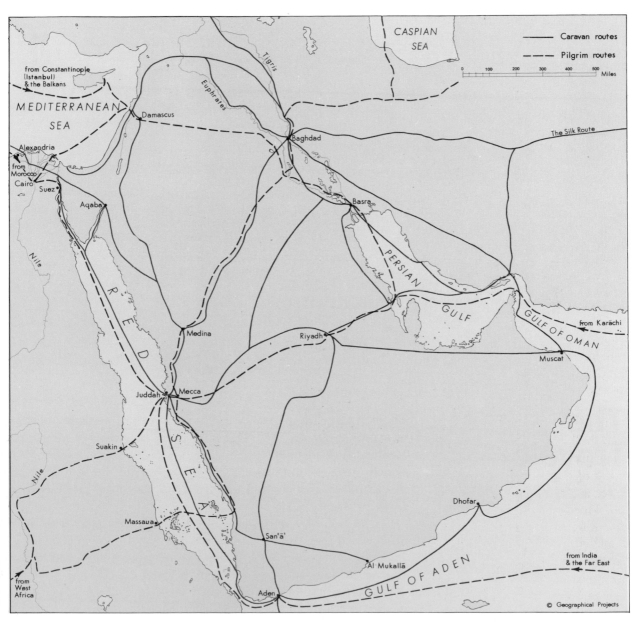

القص والجبال والنبى والله انها لفظت على بالله فاضاعت من زجها

شد من زجهالماداني قرنت بالرقعة درهما وقطعة وقلت لها ان رغبت فى المشوف المعلم

رن الى الدرهم فوصى بالسر المعم وان اب ان ان نرجع خذ نذى القطعة واسبرجن

ن الى استخلاض البدر بالتم والابلج الهم وقالت دع جدالك ينبلغ عما بد لك فاسقطه

The Traveler of Islam

2

The first travelers in Arabia to leave any record of their journeys were Moslems making the pilgrimage to the holy cities of Mecca and Medina. Their accounts of the hajj fascinated Western readers who, as non-Moslems, were forbidden to take part in the Moslem ceremonies. They also inspired Europeans to try to see the forbidden cities for themselves.

One of the most remarkable of the Moslem travelers was Sheik Mohammed ibn Abdulla Ibn-Batuta, who was born in Tangier in 1304. Ibn-Batuta came from a family of religious judges, and he had studied theology and law in Tangier before he decided to make the pilgrimage. Although the pilgrimage was above all a religious duty, it also provided Ibn-Batuta with an opportunity to broaden his

education. By talking and studying with the scholars he met on his journey, he would fit himself to assume the duties of a magistrate when he returned to Tangier. In June, 1325, the 21-year-old pilgrim said good-by to his parents and set off for Arabia.

Money seems to have been no problem for Ibn-Batuta. Apparently, his family was well enough known in the Arab world to ensure that he would be introduced not only to scholars but also to the powerful rulers who could help to make his journey easier. And he himself soon seems to have become an experienced traveler. He did, of course, have the advantage of being an educated young man from the "Far West." As such, he was an object of curiosity and interest, and someone to be welcomed and entertained.

Above left: the color and splendor of life in the Moslem world, remarkable to European travelers, would have seemed normal to Ibn-Batuta. Here, an Arabian miniature shows a group of Middle Eastern horsemen.

Above: another illustration from the same manuscript, dated 1237. Some of the riders are mounted on camels—the most usual form of transport in Arabia.

19

Above: a water hole in the wastes of Arabia. Desert travel can still be hazardous—note the cartridge belts worn by the men. The woman, like all nomads, has her wealth in portable form—her beautiful silver ornaments.

From his lively *Travels* we do not only learn about the religious ceremonies of the hajj. Ibn-Batuta also includes his impressions of the people he met and of the towns and cities he visited. He gives details about food and traveling conditions and the different kinds of trade and business carried on throughout Arabia.

When Ibn-Batuta first set out from Tangier in 1325, he traveled along the North African coast road to Alexandria. From there, he went south to Cairo and Upper Egypt where he hoped he would be able to board a boat to cross the Red Sea. But because of a local war in that part of Egypt, he had to return down the Nile River and make his way to Damascus. There he could join a pilgrim caravan for the journey to the holy cities.

It was early August, 1326, by the time Ibn-Batuta actually reached Damascus, a city which, like many other travelers, he found more beautiful than any other he visited. Perhaps his enthusiasm may have been partly due to the fact that he got married there. It must have been a whirlwind courtship because on September 1 the pilgrim caravan left the city for the hajj.

Right: a group of camels with their herder, a woman. Among the nomads of the desert, it is the women who do all the heavy work, even to taking down and putting up the tents when the nomads strike camp, and move on.

This army of thousands of pilgrims made its way southeastward behind the coastal mountains of present-day Syria and Jordan. South of Damascus the caravan stopped for four days at Al Karak so that the travelers could rest and prepare themselves for the terrible heat of the desert. At Tabūk, 200 miles farther south, the caravan started to make forced marches, traveling night and day to reduce the time from one water hole to the next. At the Wadi al Ukhaydir, Ibn-Batuta was told a frightening story about a caravan which had passed through the valley in a previous year. Apparently a particularly dry wind had dried up the water supplies in the oases, and hundreds of people had died of thirst.

Five days' journey from the Wadi al Ukhaydir, which Ibn-Batuta appropriately referred to as the valley of hell, the caravan reached Medā'in Sālih. At Medā'in Sālih, there was an abundant supply of water, yet the pilgrims would not drink. They believed that Mohammed had once ridden his camel through Medā'in Sālih without stopping and had forbidden his followers to waste time by stopping to drink there. Ibn Batuta was amazed at this strange custom on the part of the pilgrims, though other travelers do not mention it.

From Medā'in Sālih it was another half day's journey through the

Above: a plan of the Kaaba enclosure in Mecca, painted on a Turkish tile in the 1600's. The Kaaba, or Cubical House, is the central point of the whole Moslem pilgrimage. It is Moslem belief that Abraham and his son Ishmael built the Kaaba on the site of the house where Hagar and Ishmael lived after their flight into the desert.

desert to the oasis of Al 'Ula where the pilgrims were allowed to drink and rest. The caravan remained several days there, while everyone washed their clothes and replenished their meager supplies. Three days later they arrived at Medina, where they worshiped at the mosque where Mohammed is buried.

Shortly after leaving Medina, the caravan stopped for the pilgrims to change into the *ihram,* the special garment worn by all Moslems making the pilgrimage. The ihram consists of two pieces of white cotton cloth which are wrapped around the body. When they had put on the ihram, the pilgrims were ready to begin the final stage of the journey to Mecca. Although Ibn-Batuta writes in great detail about the various rituals of the hajj, he also found time to observe the people of Mecca. He was greatly impressed by the elegance of the merchants in the holy city, and he thought the women were beautiful, chaste, and pious. He was overwhelmed by the sweet scent they left behind them as they moved about, and explains that these women would go without food in order to save money to buy perfumes. Then every Thursday night—the eve of the Moslem

Above: a frankincense tree in Dhofar, in the south of the Arabian Peninsula. Left: a closer view of a branch showing how the bark is cut away to let the resin seep out. The resin is milky at first, and hardens into pale drops (called *tears*) after two to three months' exposure to the air. These tears are burned as incense.

23

Sabbath—they would come to the mosque wearing their finest clothes and saturated with exotic perfume.

By mid-November, 1326, Ibn-Batuta was ready to leave Mecca. He had already made friends with the commander of the caravan which would go northeast to Baghdad, and was therefore able to travel under his protection. A vast number of pilgrims traveled with the Baghdad caravan. Groups of peddlars accompanied the caravan, so that the pilgrims could buy food and the few necessities they needed along the way. When the caravan entered the Nejd, it stopped at a *birka*—a reservoir—that had been built for the use of pilgrims in the early 800's. Even today this reservoir is used by the Bedouin tribesmen to water their camels.

When the caravan arrived in Baghdad, Ibn-Batuta decided that he would continue his travels through the Middle East. From then on it is more difficult to follow his exact route. According to his journal, in 1327 he was back again in Mecca where he stayed for three years. He also made a short trip to East Africa and then returned again to Arabia to visit Yemen. Ibn-Batuta got as far up into the mountains of this region as the ancient city of Ṣanʿāʾ. He then returned to the coast at Aden.

From Aden, Ibn-Batuta made his way to eastern Africa but he later returned to Arabia and traveled along the south coast to Dhofar. Like many other travelers in the area he commented on the incense trade. At the port of Hasik there were a great number of frankincense trees. Ibn Batuta explains that these trees have "thin leaves out of which drips, when they are slashed, sap like milk. This turns into a gum, which is the frankincense." Another thing which impressed him at Hasik was the dependence of the local people on the fish they caught. These were called *lukham* and were like a dogfish. When these fish had been sliced open and dried in the sun they were eaten. The bones were saved, and used by the people to weave flimsy coverings for the walls of their primitive huts.

Ibn-Batuta continued following the Arabian coast to Oman and then around into the Persian Gulf. At Bahrain, he prepared for his third journey to Mecca, this time traveling westward across the peninsula. At Mecca, this restless and inquisitive young man decided to prolong his travels. He visited central Asia, India and even China before, some 15 years later, he made his way home to Tangier.

Ibn-Batuta's journal reflects in great detail the Arab world of the mid-1300's. It was, for him, an ordered world, where an educated young man could move about with great freedom and in safety. The explorers who followed him into the Arabian Peninsula found it a far more hazardous place.

Right: in the Persian Gulf, on the island of Bahrain, a fisherman casts his net. More than 600 years ago, Ibn-Batuta would have seen fishermen casting their nets just like this.

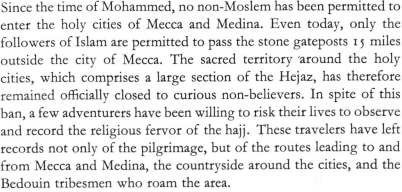

Left: the prophet Mohammed, ascending to a welcoming heaven on his donkey al-Burak. The picture comes from a Persian manuscript of about 1540.

Since the time of Mohammed, no non-Moslem has been permitted to enter the holy cities of Mecca and Medina. Even today, only the followers of Islam are permitted to pass the stone gateposts 15 miles outside the city of Mecca. The sacred territory around the holy cities, which comprises a large section of the Hejaz, has therefore remained officially closed to curious non-believers. In spite of this ban, a few adventurers have been willing to risk their lives to observe and record the religious fervor of the hajj. These travelers have left records not only of the pilgrimage, but of the routes leading to and from Mecca and Medina, the countryside around the cities, and the Bedouin tribesmen who roam the area.

The first non-Moslem known to have visited the holy cities was an Italian, Ludovico di Varthema. He wrote a book about his travels, which was published in Rome in 1510. In it, he recounts his adventures in Egypt, Syria, the Hejaz, and Yemen. He also describes his subsequent journeys in India, and eastward as far as the Spice Islands (the Moluccas).

Like Ibn-Batuta's story, Di Varthema's book has the liveliness and fascination of an adventure novel. In it he writes little about his family or early life. All we know is that he lived in Bologna and had probably been a soldier before deciding to become a traveler. He was obviously a man of spirit and boldness, who wanted to see faraway lands, and win the kind of fame which explorers could achieve at that time. Unlike Ibn Batuta, Di Varthema was not a learned man. He describes himself as "of very slender understanding" and not given to study. In his own words, he resolved to see things "personally and with my own eyes, to endeavor to ascertain the situation of places, the qualities of people, the diversities of animals, the varieties of the fruit-bearing and odoriferous trees—remembering well that the testimony of one eyewitness is worth more than ten thousand hearsays."

Above: Di Varthema presenting his book to the Countess of Albi, to whom it is dedicated, from the German edition of 1515. It is possible that the artist of the woodcuts in this edition had seen Di Varthema, as in each he is recognizably the same person, wearing a goatee beard.

Early in 1503, Di Varthema arrived in Alexandria in Egypt and from there went on to Cairo. He then made his way to Beirut and Damascus, where he seems to have picked up a working knowledge of Arabic. It was April, 1503, when he arrived at Damascus, and the hajj caravan was preparing for the annual pilgrimage. In the early 1500's, a tough and well-armed escort was necessary to protect the pilgrims from the Bedouin raiders who followed the caravan. The Bedouins would often attack the pilgrims and camels when they

Above: Mamelukes exercising in front of a palace in Cairo. The Mamelukes first came to Egypt as prisoners of war. Originally from Europe and Circassia, they were converted to Islam, and became enormously powerful. In 1250, they seized control of Egypt, and they ruled the country until 1517.

stopped at an oasis to refresh themselves. Ibn-Batuta had not mentioned this particular danger, which suggests that the Bedouins had become more hostile toward strangers in the 200 years since he traveled on the same road. Di Varthema made friends with the captain of the Mameluke escort which was to accompany the caravan to Mecca. Using his wits, and perhaps some money in the form of bribes, he managed to persuade the Mamelukes to allow him to enrol as one of them.

In Di Varthema's time, the Mamelukes, from whose ranks the escorts for the pilgrim caravans were drawn, ruled over the lands of Egypt and Syria. Originally, however, they had come to Egypt as prisoners of war from Europe and Circassia (the southern part of Russia). Converted to Islam, the Mamelukes gradually rose to power in the government service, and in A.D. 1250, they seized control of Egypt. From Di Varthema's point of view, one of their most important characteristics was that, although as Moslems they could make the pilgrimage, they did not necessarily look like Arabs. In the

Mameluke guard, Di Varthema could join the hajj with little fear of detection.

When he enrolled in the guard, Di Varthema took the Arabic name of Yunos, and obtained a uniform and a horse. It was an enormous caravan that started on the 40-day march to the holy cities—according to Di Varthema, there were 40,000 pilgrims, 35,000 camels, and a Mameluke escort of 60.

One of the most interesting parts of Di Varthema's journal is an account of the caravan's first stopping place inside the Hejaz region, at the oasis of Khaybar. For many centuries, there had been a Jewish colony there, perhaps founded after the destruction of Judea by Nebuchadnezzar II in the 500's B.C., and colonized by refugees from subsequent disasters.

Di Varthema describes the mountainous oasis as being 10 or 12 miles in circumference with a community of between 4,000 and 5,000 people "who go naked and are in height five or six spans [about four feet], and have a feminine voice and are more black than any other color. They live entirely on the flesh of sheep and eat nothing else. They are circumcised and confess that they are Jews; and if they can get a Moor [Arab] into their hands they skin him alive."

At Khaybar, Di Varthema was also impressed by seeing eight

Right: the battle for a water hole in which Di Varthema reports that 1,600 Bedouins were killed by the caravan's Mameluke guard. Di Varthema says that the water hole was in the valley of Sodom and Gomorrah, which he describes as truly desert and barren. According to the Bible, the cities were destroyed because of the wickedness of their inhabitants.

Above: Di Varthema's caravan on
its way to Mecca. Di Varthema says
of the group: "The pilgrims travel
with wives and children and houses
like a Turkish tent made from wool. . . .
The caravan was going in two groups . . .
60 of them Mamelukes for saving the
people. One part of the Mamelukes
were going first, another one in the
middle and the third part behind the
group. We traveled night and day."

beautiful thornbushes, and two turtledoves fluttering above them.
This was like a miracle, he says, because the caravan had traveled for
16 days and nights without having seen a single animal or bird.

Eventually, the caravan reached Medina. There, the pilgrims
prayed at Mohammed's tomb—a substantial building which Di
Varthema carefully described in order to disprove the medieval
legend that Mohammed's coffin was suspended in the air by giant
magnets. Soon after leaving the city, the caravan stopped for a day
to give the pilgrims time to bathe and put on the ihram, just as
Ibn-Batuta had described.

Di Varthema traveled on with the hajj to Mecca. There he was
careful to write down all sorts of details, not only of the religious
ceremonies, but of the city itself and the trade which went on there.
Moslems from many Eastern countries were gathered in Mecca in
that May of 1503—Indians, Persians, Syrians, Ethiopians. All of
them had come as pilgrims on the hajj, but some were more interested
in the possibilities of trade than in the religious festivities.

About 10 miles east of Mecca is the sacred Mount Arafat where
part of the Moslem ceremonies took place. At the foot of the
mountain were two reservoirs, one for the caravan from Cairo and
the other for the one from Damascus. The Cairo caravan was far
larger than the Damascus one, with 64,000 camels accompanying
the pilgrims and an escort of 100 Mamelukes. The ceremonies at

the mountain included the sacrifice of at least two sheep for every pilgrim. The meat was given to the poor, and Di Varthema thought that more people came because they were hungry, than wanted to take part in the ceremonies.

When the caravan returned north to Damascus, Di Varthema decided to desert the Mameluke guard. This was a dangerous move and could be punishable by death. The Mameluke officers had no intention of allowing deserters from the escort to wander about in Arabia as they wished. Besides, Di Varthema was in danger of being killed as a non-Moslem in the holy city. However, he soon thought of a way to extricate himself from this tight corner. The Arabs were at that time badly in need of guns to use against the Portuguese, whose ships were beginning to divert the profitable trade between India and Europe around Africa and away from Arabia. Di Varthema managed to convince a merchant that he was a skilfull maker of cannon, and was allowed to hide in his house.

When the pilgrim caravans and the Mamelukes had left Mecca, Di Varthema ventured on to Juddah, the port of Mecca. Juddah too was a dangerous place for a Mameluke deserter. There the Italian hid himself in a mosque. He pretended to be very ill and lay groaning among the large group of beggars who had also found shelter there. In the evening he would steal out to buy food and observe the goings on in the busy port.

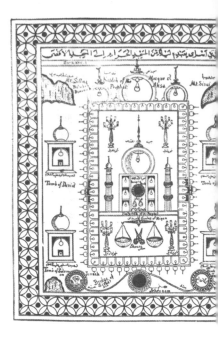

After three weeks in hiding, Di Varthema managed to get a place on a ship bound for Persia that stopped along the coast of Yemen and docked at Aden. There, Di Varthema experienced his first real misfortune. The Arabs of Yemen were suspicious of any outsider whom they thought might be a spy for the Portuguese traders. Perhaps because his disguise seemed less credible than in Mecca, the Italian spent several months in jail. But afterwards he managed to travel inland in Yemen and reached as far up in the mountains as Ṣanʻāʼ.

After his visit to Ṣanʻāʼ, Di Varthema returned to Aden where he was again forced to hide in a mosque during the day. He nevertheless managed to get himself a place on a ship which was going to Persia and then on to India. By 1510, he had apparently made his way home to Italy, because in that year the book of his travels was published.

Nearly 200 years passed before the next recorded visit of a European to Mecca. This was made by Joseph Pitts, an English

Below: a lone rider on the coastal plain north of Juddah. Di Varthema would have made this part of his journey equally alone—he deserted the Mameluke guard in Mecca and traveled on to Juddah by himself.

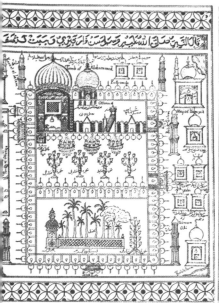
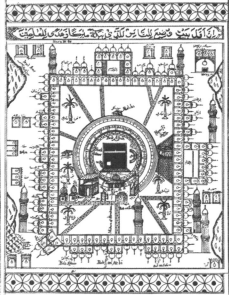
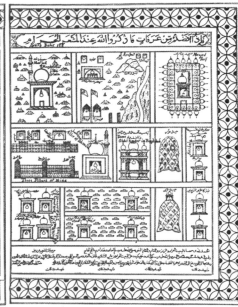

seaman who, in 1678, was captured by Barbary pirates off the north coast of Africa. Pirates in those days often kept their prisoners for years. Pitts, who was later sold as a slave to a Moslem cavalry officer, did not make the pilgrimage until 1685. By the time he accompanied his master to Mecca, he could speak both Arabic and Turkish. He had also been forced to become a Moslem. Having observed and recorded the various stages of the pilgrimage, Pitts managed to escape and eventually returned home. Once back in England, he wrote a book about his adventures.

The next known European visitor to Mecca was a mysterious Spaniard, who called himself Ali Bey. He made the pilgrimage in 1801. Ali Bey not only knew Arabic, but was also trained in geology and botany. He took scientific instruments on his journey and, surprisingly, he managed to use them without arousing the suspicions of the inhabitants of Mecca. His principal contribution to exploration was that he fixed the position of Mecca by astronomical observation.

Eight years later, in 1809, Ulrich Jaspar Seetzen, a German botanist, made a journey to Mecca disguised as a Moslem. He had already spent some years traveling in the Middle East, and had a thorough knowledge of Arabic. From Mecca, Seetzen went on to Medina, and then to Al Mukhā. Unfortunately, soon afterward his disguise must have aroused suspicion and, in 1811, he was murdered somewhere near Ta'izz.

During the 300 years between Di Varthema's visit to Mecca and Seetzen's travels in Arabia, the political situation in and around the Arabian Peninsula had altered greatly. The Turks had extended the Ottoman Empire to include Iraq, Syria, Palestine, Egypt, the north coast of Africa, and the Hejaz, but they did not penetrate the heart of Arabia. In the 1500's, the Portuguese seized the island of

Above: the Mecca certificate, given to pilgrims to the sacred city. It shows the landmarks of the pilgrimage. As every true Moslem is commanded to make at least one pilgrimage to Mecca during his life, if it is at all possible, this certificate is looked on almost as a passport to heaven. Below: Ali Bey, said to have been a Moslem prince, son of Othman Bey.

Above: Ulrich Jaspar Seetzen, a German botanist. Seetzen visited Mecca, but was later murdered near Ta'izz.

Socotra off the southern coast of Arabia, and established a base at Muscat, and one farther east at Hormuz on the Persian Gulf.

By the end of the 1500's, Portuguese power had begun to decline. The Dutch, the British, and the French began to push eastward into the Indian Ocean and the Pacific to acquire new territory and build up overseas empires. The Red Sea and the Persian Gulf were frequently visited by ships of the British, Dutch, and French East India companies, which used to call at the major ports in Arabia. But few of the men on these ships ventured farther inland than the warehouse areas in the ports.

Inside Arabia itself, important religious and political developments had taken place. These developments had their root in a reformation of Islam, which involved a return to the simple practices and teachings of Mohammed. The movement was led by Abd al-Wahhab and sprang up in the district of al-Ared (in the southern part of the Nejd in which lies the present-day town of Riyadh).

In the mid-1700's, Abd al-Wahhab had been taken under the protection and patronage of Mohammed al-Saud, head of the Saudi family, which ruled the area around Dar'iyah. In 1745, he founded the Wahhabi sect, and preached the reformation of Islam. His religious message strengthened the Saudis in their rivalry with neighboring chiefs. Every campaign fought by the recently converted tribesmen against a rival state became a holy war.

Through Mohammed al-Saud, the Wahhabis became the masters of the Nejd. His son, Saud bin Abdelaziz al Saud, also played a part in enlarging the Wahhabi empire, entering and capturing the Hejaz in 1802. The Wahhabis subsequently expanded their authority up to Damascus and even seized Mecca and Medina. At this point the Sultan of Turkey became alarmed about the Wahhabi movement, which threatened both the Ottoman Empire and his own religious position as Caliph of Islam. He ordered the governor of Egypt, Mohammed Ali Pasha, to deal with the situation.

In 1812, an Egyptian army drove the Wahhabis out of Mecca and Medina. Six years later the Egyptians heavily defeated the Wahhabis at Dar'iyah, and then reduced the Saudi capital to a state of ruin. The power of the Saudi family was broken and the Wahhabi empire ceased to exist. But the religious fervor of the Wahhabi religion survived among some of the tribes. It was to be a factor in the eventual revival of the powerful Saudi family in the late 1800's.

LIBEDIA·

While the Egyptian campaign against the Wahhabis was at its height, a Swiss explorer, John Lewis Burckhardt, arrived in Juddah, the port of Mecca. His aim was to make the pilgrimage to Mecca. Burckhardt traveled disguised as a Turk, calling himself Ibrahim ibn Abdullah. He spoke excellent Arabic, knew the teachings of the Koran (the Moslem holy book), and, as a last resort, could claim to be a convert to Islam, though it is not clear if indeed he was.

Burckhardt had been employed to seek the sources of the Niger River by a society in London called the Association for Promoting the Discovery of the Interior Parts of Africa. But, while waiting for a caravan at Cairo, he had decided to explore further in the Middle East before resuming his mission.

Burckhardt traveled about in the Hejaz and made a detailed account of everything he saw and heard in Arabia. He was a careful man, little impressed by the kind of adventures which had carried Di Varthema from place to place, and was content to go about unnoticed while he made notes for his journal. Burckhardt was the supreme observer not only of the hajj, but of all aspects of the religious and secular world he visited. His journal is among the most complex documents about the holy cities. Long after it was

Above: one of the Portuguese forts along the Arabian coast. When Portuguese ships sailed regularly to India by the sea route round the Cape of Good Hope, the Portuguese built forts to safeguard the route in strategic places along the coast. But the Portuguese never settled inland.

35

Below: Selim III, Sultan of Turkey 1789–1807. It was during his reign that the fanatical Wahhabis began to take over much of Arabia.

published, explorers, students of religion, and anyone interested in the Arabian country and in the politics, history, and commercial life of the area during this period found it essential reading.

After spending a year in Arabia, Burckhardt returned to Cairo, hoping this time to meet up with a caravan to take him into the Sahara. There he rested and made some final notes about his Arabian travels. He was also convalescing from dysentery, which he had caught during his stay in Medina. And, before the next caravan was ready to depart for the interior, Burckhardt died from another bout of this deadly disease. It was characteristic of him that before his death he had mailed the manuscript of his journal to his patrons in London.

The next European visitor to Mecca and Medina had read and been fascinated by Burckhardt's journal. This was an Englishman, Richard Burton, who made the pilgrimage in 1853. He traveled disguised not as a convert to Islam but as a born Moslem. Burton had an extraordinary facility for learning languages. At the age of 21

Above: John Lewis Burckhardt, the Swiss explorer, in the Moslem dress in which he disguised himself for the journey to Mecca. He was a careful observer and kept a detailed journal.

Above right: Petra, an ancient ruined city in what is now Jordan. David Roberts based this picture on drawings that Burckhardt himself had made.

he had landed in Bombay, India, as an army lieutenant and spent the next seven years there learning Persian and Arabic, as well as various local Indian dialects. It was during this period that he first decided upon his scheme for making the pilgrimage. In the autumn of 1852, Burton returned to London and secured a year's leave from the army and the promise of some money for his exploration from the Royal Geographical Society.

In April, 1853, Burton was ready to start for Mecca, pretending to be an Afghan pilgrim and doctor. He hoped that as a doctor he would be able to observe the details of Arab family life.

Some of Burton's trickiest moments came at the start of the

Above: the temples and rock tombs at Petra today. The carvings now seem somewhat more eroded, but they still show the amazing accuracy of Burckhardt's thorough reports on the places he visited. The city of Petra was once a flourishing trading center, but the area around the ruins is now inhabited mainly by bands of nomads.

journey. At Suez, for instance, his companions found a sextant among his belongings, not the kind of thing that a genuine pilgrim was likely to be carrying. A boy in the group accused Burton of being an infidel. Burton ruefully threw away his sextant and, to restore the confidence of his Moslem companions, "prayed five times a day for nearly a week." It seems fairly clear that the Moslems who were suspicious of Burton were also aware that he was carrying with him a good deal of money, and they hoped to benefit from some of it. "The scene ended," reports Burton, "with a general abuse of the acute youth."

At Al Wajh on the Red Sea coast, Burton's identity was again

39

Left: the fez that Burton wore. He was particularly fond of assuming native costumes and took great care to make himself as indistinguishable as possible from the local people.

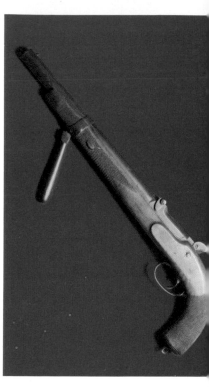

Above: Richard Burton (1821-1890). painted by Frederic Leighton in 1876. With his flair for languages and his enthusiasm for blending into an exotic background, Burton was one of the most flamboyant of the Arabian explorers.

Above right: Burton's pistol. Had Burton carried such a weapon openly when he made the pilgrimage to Mecca, his companions would certainly have suspected that he was not a dervish.

questioned. A number of Moslems were lounging about at a coffee house—"lying down, smoking, drinking water, bathing, and picking their teeth with their daggers." Among them was an inquisitive man who called himself a Pathan (a person of Afghan stock, living on the borders of Pakistan and Afghanistan). "He could speak five or six languages, he knew a number of people everywhere, and he had traveled far and wide over Central Asia. These fellows are always good detectors of an incognito. I avoided answering his questions about my native place . . . I asked him, when he insisted upon my having been born somewhere, to guess for himself. To my joy he claimed me for a brother Pathan. . . . We then sat smoking with 'effusion' . . ."

Burton gives a particularly vivid account of the pilgrim ship that carried them from Suez to Yanbu', the port of Medina. Named the *Silk al-Zahab* (golden wire) the ship had two masts—but only one with a sail—and no deck, except at the stern which was high enough to act as a sail in a gale of wind. "She had no means of reefing, no compass, no log, no sounding lines, no spare ropes, nor even the suspicion of a chart." On boarding her, Burton explains, the first thing to be done after gaining standing room was to fight for greater comfort. "In a few minutes nothing was to be seen but a confused mass of humanity, each item indiscriminately punching and pulling, scratching and biting, butting and trampling, with cries of rage and all the accompaniments of a proper fray." Burton and his companions eventually triumphed over the opposition, composed mainly of North African pilgrims, and arranged themselves reasonably comfortably.

During the journey down the Red Sea the *Silk al-Zahab* kept close to the coast. Every night the ship anchored to allow the pilgrims to sleep on dry land. One evening, while wading to the shore, Burton felt the acute pain of something running into his toe. He extracted what seemed to be a piece of thorn, but, by the time the ship reached Yanbu', he could hardly put his foot to the ground. This accident meant that he had to make the long, slow, bandit-threatened trip to Medina and Mecca in a *shugduf,* a sort of cot slung along the side of a camel like a pannier. What Burton thought was a thorn turned out to be the spine of a sea urchin, a type of small sea animal. This unfortunate accident put an end to Burton's ambitious plan of

Above: the ihram, the costume worn by the pilgrims to Mecca. While wearing the ihram, the pilgrim must follow strict rules of ritual purification. Below: boats like those the pilgrims would use to reach the Arabian coast.

crossing Arabia after he had made the pilgrimage to the holy cities.

Burton's journey from Medina to Mecca was by an inland route not previously reported by a European. But there was nothing geographically new about it. From the point of view of exploration, this great adventurer's Arabian travels were one of his lesser achievements. The brilliance of Burton's journey to Mecca was his faultless disguise and his journal, *Personal Narrative of a Pilgrimage to Al-Medinah and Meccah.* His account, for instance, of his first sight of the Kaaba, housing the sacred Black Stone, shrouded in the black cloth *kiswah,* conveys with conviction one of the supreme moments of his pilgrimage. "There at last it lay, the bourn [object] of my long and weary pilgrimage ... I may truly say that, of all the worshippers who clung weeping to the curtain, or who pressed their beating hearts to the stone, none felt for the moment a deeper emotion than did the Haji [pilgrim] from the far-north. It was as if the legends of the Arabs spoke truth, and that the waving wings of Angels, not the sweet breeze of morning, were agitating and swelling the black covering of the shrine. But, to confess the humbling truth, theirs was the high feeling of religious enthusiasm, mine was the ecstasy of gratified pride."

In 1908–1909, another Englishman, A. J. B. Wavell, repeated Burton's feat of making the journey to Mecca and Medina in disguise. Wavell traveled as a Zanzibari pilgrim. Perhaps the unique aspect of his journey was that he traveled on the recently completed Hejaz Railway from Damascus to Medina. The building of a railroad for the pilgrims had been sponsored by the Ottoman sultan, Abdul-Hamid II and had been financed by subscriptions from every part of the Moslem world. Although it was intended to make the pilgrimage safer and easier, the railroad was at the same time strategically useful to the Ottoman Empire. The Ottoman Turks were at that time having to defend Syria and the Hejaz against the advances of the British. Besides, they were constantly harassed by the Bedouins of Arabia who never ceased their opposition to Turkish rule.

The rail distance between Damascus and Medina was over 1,000 miles. It took four days—a remarkably short time when compared with the 30 or 40 days it took for the journey by caravan. The train was extremely crowded, and many pilgrims who did not try to board it until the last minute were turned away. Sitting opposite

Above: a cartoon of Burton in 1882, captioned "Captain Burton, our uncommercial traveller." Behind him are Baedeker and Murray—both of whom wrote notable guidebooks in the 1800's —lamenting that Burton got there first.

Wavell and his traveling friends in the train were two Turks, father and son, whose only luggage appeared to consist of a phonograph. This was apparently a popular innovation to the other passengers in the car who were eager to listen to recordings of passages from the Koran.

Added to the unpleasantness of overcrowded conditions in the train was the danger of attack by Bedouins. The tribesmen resented the railroad because of their vested interest in camel transportation and the old pilgrim caravans. From Medā'in Sālih onward the railroad stations had to be guarded by Turkish garrisons. But the crowded train carrying Wavell's party arrived safely at Medina.

From Medina to Yanbu', Wavell and his companions traveled in the traditional way, with a camel caravan. At Yanbu' they boarded a steamer, another innovation, which conveyed them south to Juddah. At Mecca they began the pilgrimage, which in all took five days. As usual this involved a trek to Mount Arafat, and like almost all the Europeans who preceded him, Wavell was particularly impressed by this part of the hajj: "At least half a million people are traversing these nine miles of road between sunrise and ten o'clock this day; about half of them are mounted, and many of them possess baggage-animals as well. The roar of this great column is like a breaking sea, and the dust spreads for miles over the surrounding country. When, passing through the second defile, we came

Above: a picture of a *takhtrawan*, a grandee's litter, from Burton's book, *Personal Narrative of a Pilgrimage to Al-Medinah and Meccah*. Burton reported that the pilgrims traveled on foot or on camel. The wealthy were borne in these splendid litters, with a horse saddled ready for the grandee should he decide to leave his litter.

Right: a station under construction
on the Hejaz Railway. The Pilgrimage
was a difficult and often dangerous
journey, and the railroad was built
to make it easier for the pilgrims.
However, the Bedouin tribesmen who
had an interest in the camel caravans
resented the railroad, and they often
used to attack the passing trains.

Below: Kasim Pasha, director in chief
of the construction of the railroad.

in sight of Arafat itself, the spectacle was stranger still. The hill was literally black with people, and tents were springing up round it, hundreds to the minute, in an ever-widening circle. As we approached, the dull murmur caused by thousands of people shouting the formula, 'Lebeka lebeka, Allohooma lebeka,' which had long been audible, became so loud that it dominated every other sound. In the distance it had sounded rather ominous, suggestive of some deep disturbance of great power, like the rumble of an earthquake."

In spite of the innovations of railroad and steamer, the pilgrimage to Mecca changed little between the time Di Varthema joined the

Above: A. J. B. Wavell in Damascus in 1908. Like Burton, he made the trip to Mecca disguised as a pilgrim.

hajj and Wavell's visit to the holy cities 400 years later. Travel was perhaps easier, but the dangers of discovery were just as great, and each of the travelers was aware that his life was staked on the effectiveness of his disguise. But, far from deterring travelers, the dangers of visiting the forbidden cities actually attracted adventurers to Arabia—their stories of the hajj, of the holy cities, and of Arabian life fascinated Europeans and gave them a glimpse of the beliefs and customs of the Moslem world. And in their attempts to follow routes previously known only to the Moslem pilgrims, these bold men carried out the first exploration of the Hejaz.

Arabia Felix
4

Many explorers have found the southwest corner of Arabia the most fascinating part of the whole country. This mountainous region consists of two main areas—Yemen, facing the Red Sea in the west, and the Hadhramaut country, which faces the Gulf of Aden in the south. It is an area of extraordinary natural beauty, from the high mountains of Yemen to the deep gorge of the Wadi Hadhramaut. But much of its appeal for travelers lies in its ancient history.

From about 1400 B.C., a flourishing civilization existed in Yemen. The country's first capital was at Main. Then, in 950 B.C., a tribe called the Sabaeans invaded the fertile Yemen uplands and established their capital city at Marib, the legendary capital of the Queen of Sheba. The Sabaeans were succeeded by the Himyarites who moved the capital to Zafar, south of the modern city of Ṣan'ā'. The three ancient kingdoms are usually referred to collectively as the Sabaeans, and their language as Himyaritic.

At the time of the Sabaean kingdoms, Yemen was immensely rich in agriculture and natural resources, adorned with fine temples and palaces. But above all, the Sabaeans traded in myrrh, frankincense, cinnamon, and numerous other aromatic herbs. These spices and herbs were in great demand in the Middle East and Europe for making perfumes and ointments and for burning as incense at religious ceremonies. The route by which they were exported became known as the Incense Trail, and the rich trade in these treasures led European writers to call the southwestern part of Arabia, and Yemen in particular, *Arabia Felix*—which in Latin means happy, or fortunate, Arabia.

In the mid-1700's, however, little was yet known about the history of Yemen. For centuries, geographers, explorers, and scholars had speculated about the country. They knew something about it from references in the Old Testament and classical literature. But it was not until 1759 that an expedition was organized to visit Arabia—and in particular Yemen—with the hope of learning more about its history, and about the land itself.

Left: a hill tribesman, from the Hadhramaut region in southern Arabia, sits on a barren ledge overlooking the vast natural chasm of a wadi spread far beneath his feet.

47

Above: Carsten Niebuhr, the German explorer who was the only member of the Danish expedition of 1761 to return to Europe. Although there was no official leader of the group. Niebuhr's force of character and his methodical scholarship—as well as the fact that he survived to report the group's findings —made him outstanding among the expedition members.

Above right: a dagger and sheath that Niebuhr brought back from his travels.

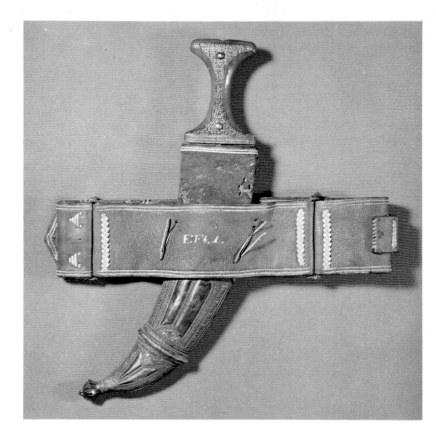

The idea for a scientific expedition to increase European knowledge of pre-Islamic Arabia was suggested to King Frederik of Denmark by a Hebrew scholar called Johann David Michaelis from Göttingen in Germany. The king showed his interest in the scheme by drawing up a list of instructions for the explorers. He also made arrangements for a ship to be fitted out. Five scholars, each one an expert in his particular field, were selected for the expedition. The project was patronized and financed by King Frederik, but the men who made up the party came from Germany, Sweden, and Denmark. Carsten Niebuhr, the mathematician and surveyor, was from northern Germany; William Baurenfeind, the artist, was from southern Germany. Peter Forskål, the botanist, and Berggren, their European servant, were Swedes. The two Danes were Friedrich Christian von Haven, a philologist and Oriental scholar, and Christian Carl Kramer, a surgeon and zoologist.

Below: a farmer from the Yemen high-lands, with a dagger and sheath very similar to the one that Niebuhr brought back from Arabia over 200 years ago.

Above: William Baurenfeind, the artist on the Danish expedition, in an engraving taken from a self-portrait. Baurenfeind died on board the ship taking the party to India.

There was to be no official leader of King Frederik's expedition—each man was to pursue the area of inquiry for which he was best qualified. It is difficult, however, not to think of the Danish expedition as Carsten Niebuhr's. Niebuhr proved himself a man of quite exceptional intelligence and character. And he was the only member of the party to return safely to Europe.

The expedition sailed from Copenhagen for the Mediterranean Sea in January, 1761. The party then made a short trip through Alexandria and Suez to Mount Sinai, later returning to Suez. From Suez, they sailed to Juddah where they arrived in October, 1762.

After remaining there for six weeks, the men boarded another ship to take them on to Al Luhayyah, the northernmost port of Yemen. During the 1700's, Moslem fanaticism in Yemen was at a low ebb and the members of the expedition were unmolested. They wore Arab dress, but were never required to prove that they were Moslems.

The party traveled along the coastal strip to Bayt al Faqīh, the center of the coffee trade. There, Europeans were already well known and accepted as buyers of this important Yemen product. Bayt al Faqīh was the inland depot for coffee on its way from the Yemen hills to the big ports such as Al Mukhā. Because travel was so safe, some of the members of the team ventured to go on short expeditions of their own. Forskål went up into the hills to collect herbs. Niebuhr hired a donkey to explore the Tihama—the narrow, infertile coastal plain bordering the Red Sea. On his excursions, Niebuhr was careful to dress as a poor man so as to discourage the numerous robbers who roamed the area.

"A turban, a greatcoat wanting the sleeves, a shirt, linen drawers and a pair of slippers were all the dress I wore. It being the fashion of the country to carry arms when traveling, I had a saber and pistols at my girdle. A piece of an old carpet was my saddle, and served

Above: the terraced fields of Yemen still closely resemble Niebuhr's description of them. Agricultural methods in the Yemen highlands have changed little for hundreds of years.

Above: Peter Forskål, the Swedish
botanist on the Danish expedition.
Below: a woman of Juddah selling
bread, a drawing by the German
artist, Baurenfeind. Niebuhr published
this in his account of the expedition.

me likewise for a seat at table and various other purposes. To cover me at night I had the linen cloak which the Arabs wrap about their shoulders, to shelter me from the sun and rain. A bucket of water, an article of indispensable necessity to a traveler in these arid regions, hung by my saddle. I had for some time endeavored to suit myself to the Arabian manner of living, and now could spare many conveniences to which I had become accustomed in Europe, and could content myself with bad bread, the only article to be obtained in most of the inns."

As members of the party—sometimes traveling alone and sometimes as a group—went up into the highlands of Yemen, they observed that the villages were built of stone, in contrast to the mud villages in the lowlands. They wrote, too, of the life of the industrious farmers. Niebuhr reflects upon the countryside in his account of a visit to a village called Bulgosa. "Neither asses nor mules can be used here; the hills are to be climbed by narrow and steep paths: yet, in comparison with the parched plains of Tihama, the scenery seemed to me charming. . . . The coffee trees were all in flower at Bulgosa, and exhaled an exquisitely agreeable perfume. They are planted upon terraces in the form of an amphitheater. Most of them are only watered by the rains that fall; but some, indeed, from large reservoirs upon the heights; in which spring water is collected, in order to be sprinkled upon the terraces; where the trees grow so thick together that the rays of the sun can hardly enter among their branches. We were told that those trees, thus artificially watered, yielded ripe fruit twice in the year. . . ."

Nevertheless, travel in the mountains, where the mean temperature in summer is 85–90°F, and in the Tihama, where it can get as hot as 130°F, had already begun to affect the members of the expedition. Niebuhr caught "cold"—malaria—and Von Haven was so ill that he died before they reached Al Mukhā in April, 1763. Forskål wrote uncharitably that Von Haven "by his demise" had "made the expedition incomparably easier for the rest of us. He was of a very difficult disposition."

Left: the ruins of the great dam at Marib. Only the northern and southern ends, which were fixed to the wadi wall, have survived. The northern part is flanked by a fortress, now in ruins.

The party, now reduced to five men, set out for Ṣan‘ā’, the capital of Yemen. They struggled through the fierce summer heat of the Tihama up to cool and pleasant Ta‘izz. But by the time they were ready to leave and go on to Ṣan‘ā’, Forskål himself was weak with fever and had to be lifted onto his donkey. Though the journey was through beautiful mountain country, it was an unbearable experience for them all. For Forskål in particular, the last and most terrible part of the journey was from Menzil to Yarīm. Suffering agonies of pain, he had to be lashed to the back of a baggage camel.

Forskål died at Yarīm on July 11, 1763. He was 32 years old, a man of great brilliance and promise. Niebuhr described him as the most learned man in the whole group.

The road from Menzil to Yarīm crossed a shoulder of Jebel

Above: Bab el-Yemen, the main gate of the city of Ṣan‘ā’, the capital of Yemen. It was on the grueling trip to Ṣan‘ā’ through the Yemen mountains that Peter Forskål died in 1763.

Right: a stele—a carved stone slab—the work of Sabaean artisans, dating from the A.D. 200's. It pictures worshipers before a goddess in a temple (above), and a woman reclining on a couch, attended by her servant (below).

Summara at a height of 9,000 feet, and the landscape changed suddenly as they entered the dried up plateau of central Yemen. From Ta'izz to Menzil there had been rain every day. Niebuhr says that the earth there was "covered with a charming verdure," but at Yarīm, "no rain had fallen for three months, although distant thunder had been heard almost every day. In this want of rain the locusts had multiplied prodigiously . . ."

Though ill himself, Niebuhr remained faithful to the scholarly goals of the expedition and took note of the existence of important remains near Yarīm. "At two miles distance . . . stood a once famous city Dhafar, very little of the ruins of which now remain. The first magistrate of Yarīm, however, told me that a large stone is still to be seen there with an inscription, which neither Jews nor Mahometans [Moslems] can explain. . . ." Niebuhr thought that the city was probably once the seat of the Himyarites, and that it was likely to contain Himyaritic inscriptions.

Niebuhr also reports what he had heard about Marib—sometimes called Mariabba—the old Sabaean capital. At Marib other important ruins were to be found, the most noteworthy being a great dam which had fallen into disrepair. This was one of the immense dams which had been part of the advanced and prosperous civilization of the Sabaeans.

The four remaining members of the expedition, now all suffering from fever, stumbled on to Şan'ā'. They had two days' enforced rest waiting for an audience with the *imam* (ruler), and spent them admiring the beauty of the neighborhood, where, among other things, 20 different kinds of grapes were grown. The men were well received by the imam, who urged them to stay as long as they liked. They were, however, worried by their poor health and their nerves had been shaken by the deaths of Von Haven and Forskål. They remained at Şan'ā' for only 10 days.

Nevertheless, before leaving the capital, Niebuhr took care to note down as much as he could about the plan of the city and the life of its inhabitants. One of the things which interested him most was the Jewish community of about 2,000 which had a village outside the walls of Şan'ā'. Although they were fine artisans and kept shops in Şan'ā', the Jews returned to their district at night and were generally badly treated. Niebuhr also noted that, when one Jew was found guilty of a serious crime, the whole Jewish community suffered punishment for it. On one occasion all synagogues and houses above a certain height were demolished.

It took Niebuhr and the depleted party nine grueling days to travel from Ṣanʿāʾ down into the tropical heat of Al Mukhā. In Al Mukhā all four collapsed with fever, and Kramer, Baurenfeind, and Berggren had to be carried aboard the ship which was to take them on to Bombay on the west coast of India. But a few days after sailing, Baurenfeind and Berggren died. And in February, 1764, Kramer died in Bombay.

Niebuhr was now alone. During his 14-month stay in India, he gradually regained his strength, and decided to carry out the king's instructions to return to Europe by way of Muscat, the Persian Gulf, Iraq, and Aleppo, rather than by the temptingly easy voyage around the Cape of Good Hope. On his return journey, he was the

Below: an illustration from Harris's book about his journey to Yemen. Harris was one of the few travelers to reach Ṣanʿāʾ. Here, he is being interrogated by Ahmed Feizi Pasha, the Turkish governor general at the time of Harris' visit in the 1890's.

Above: Hermann Burchardt with a coffee merchant, Caprotti, in Ṣanʿāʾ, one of a group of photographs taken before Burchardt's murder in the hazardous country surrounding the city.

only European among his traveling companions. On November 20, 1767, he rode into Copenhagen again, having been away for very nearly seven years. He was only 34 years old.

Niebuhr then set to work to make the official report on the expedition. This involved studying the observations of his dead companions and combining them with his own. His book, first published in 1772, tells of the expedition's journeys in Yemen and of Arab manners and customs. It also covers those parts of the peninsula which none of the party had visited. This section of the book is based upon information Niebuhr had gathered by talking to educated Arabs and merchants.

Although the expedition had spent less than two years in Arabia, and had not penetrated the vast unexplored interior, it had carried out King Frederik's instructions. The six men had thoroughly explored the Yemen Tihama and had gone into the lower foothills. Niebuhr had collected the most reliable information possible about the rest of the peninsula. He was the first man to observe Arabia from a scientific point of view.

Above: the Englishman G. Wyman Bury. Below: Bury pictured in Arab dress. Bury was thoroughly at home in Arabia, and took the Arab name of Abdulla Mansur, which he later used as a pseudonym for his books about Arabia.

During the years that followed Niebuhr's journey, Moslem fanaticism in Yemen increased, and travel there became increasingly dangerous for non-Moslems. And, in fact, it was more than 70 years before the next European visited the area. The first explorers of the 1800's to brave Yemen's dangers were scholars and archaeologists, who hoped that the inscriptions and ruins Niebuhr had reported finding would throw light on the still-mysterious Sabaean-Himyaritic civilization. Between 1843 and 1890, three travelers reached the Marib dam. The first was a Frenchman, Joseph Thomas Arnaud, who studied the inscriptions and carvings he found at Marib. The other two explorers—Joseph Halévy, a Frenchman, and Edward Glaser, an Austrian—traveled to Marib under the auspices of the Académie des Inscriptions et Belles Lettres in Paris. They both took copies of the inscriptions they found there. The inscriptions gathered together by these travelers added greatly to our knowledge about pre-Islamic Arabia.

Travel as far as Ṣan'ā' was, however, still dangerous. A. J. B. Wavell, who later made the pilgrimage to Mecca on the Hejaz Railway, managed to get to Ṣan'ā' in 1891, and W. B. Harris reached the city in 1892. Both were interested in the anti-Turkish revolt which flared up at that time. But Wavell was imprisoned and Harris only just escaped from ambush south of Ṣan'ā'. In 1909, the German Hermann Burchardt was murdered in the same area, exactly 98 years after Seetzen's murder near Ta'izz.

The next important explorer in Yemen was the Englishman G. Wyman Bury. Bury, who was known to the Arabs as Abdulla Mansur, had served with a British regiment in Arabia and had spent many years living with the Arabs along the coast of the Arabian Sea. Like other Englishmen who had been fascinated by Arabia, Bury preferred the wild tribesmen to the townspeople. He had an excellent knowledge of their language, and was willing to share all their hardships in order to live among them. In 1908, Bury planned an expedition to cross Yemen and proceed along the Rub' al Khali to southern Nejd, but this ambitious scheme was opposed by the Turks.

Southwestern Arabia was home to Bury, and in 1913, his English fiancée went out to Al Hudaydah for their wedding. Together the couple journeyed to Ṣan'ā' for their honeymoon. This trip, and Bury's other travels before World War I, are recorded in two books, *The Land of Uz* and *Arabia Infelix*. Bury's descriptions of the

Above: the East India Company's survey ship *Palinurus,* at anchor in the Gulf of Aqaba. The captain, Stafford Bettesworth Haines, was fascinated with the Arab world, and managed to share his enthusiasm with his officers, several of whom made journeys inland.

country still have an appealing humor. For example, when passing out of the coastal plain of Yemen and heading for the foothills, he comments: "While the morning is still grey you may hear the rapping shots of some tribal *fracas* [noisy quarrel] from the foothills, a cheery sound, denoting that the world is once more astir and taking an intelligent interest in its affairs."

No European of his time knew Yemen as Bury did. His knowledge of the Turkish administration and his understanding of the Arab tribesmen made him a most valuable intelligence officer in the Suez Canal area during World War I.

East of Yemen, along the south coast of Arabia, lie the countries that on modern maps are called Southern Yemen and Muscat and Oman. Until the 1800's, Europeans knew little about this region, known as the Hadhramaut. Burckhardt and Niebuhr had concluded that much of the interior was desert, and their theory was supported by the reports of Moslem geographers. Parts were certainly inhabited. But no one knew for certain just what the region hid.

Circumstances conspired to maintain the isolation of the Hadhramaut. As in other parts of Arabia, the Moslem tribesmen were acutely hostile toward European infidels. The Hadhramaut, too, was geographically isolated—it is cut off from the west by mountains, has few good harbors, and its northern boundary is tightly sealed

Below: an altar dating from near the time of Christ, with an inscription in Himyaritic script. This ancient alphabet is still used by the Ethiopians, but no longer by the Arabs. However, not even an Ethiopian could understand this inscription as, although he would know the letters, he would be unable to read the language.

by the uninhabited desert Rub' al Khali—the Empty Quarter.

For many years, the Arab pirates, who for centuries had operated with great success along the coasts of southern Arabia, also helped to preserve the Hadhramaut from European intrusion. At the beginning of the 1800's, however, their power on the seas began to decline. When Ibrahim Pasha of Egypt overthrew the Wahhabis in 1818, this greatly weakened the pirates as well. And when the wooden merchant vessels of former times were replaced by ironclad steamships, the pirates in their vulnerable wooden ships could no longer attack shipping with impunity. As the pirates' strength decreased, so the British government and the East India Company began to extend their influence to southern Arabia. In so doing, they paved the way for the first exploration of the Hadhramaut.

The East India Company's first move was to dispatch survey ships to the Arabian coast. The survey ships were to choose sites for coaling stations where the company's ships could refuel on their way from Suez to Bombay. One of the 50 ships was the *Palinurus*. Among its officers was James Wellsted, a pioneer of exploration in both the Hadhramaut and Oman.

Early in May, 1834, the *Palinurus* anchored near the little port of Bi'r 'Alī between a low island and a high dark cliff. Some ruins could be seen on top of the cliff, and Wellsted and a small party landed to have a look at them. They found plentiful remains of houses, walls, and towers along the shore, and a third of the way up the cliff they found inscriptions and more ruined houses. At the top of the precipice there was a massive stone tower, Husn Ghorab. This had once been an ancient port called Cana. Frankincense was brought by sea to Cana before it was taken inland to be stored at Sabbatha (now the remote village of Shabwa). In his book *Travels in Arabia,* Wellsted describes the tower as "a place of extraordinary strength ... invaluable both as a place of safe retreat and as a magazine [storehouse] for trade."

The next year, on another surveying mission, the *Palinurus* called at Belhaf, a port a little to the west of Bi'r 'Alī. Wellsted heard that there were extensive ruins some way inland, and engaged a guide to direct him to the area. On the third day of his trek, Wellsted came to a well-watered valley in the center of which was an enormous

Below: broken pieces of stonework in the Hadhramaut. Many of these fragments have inscriptions on them In the 1800's, such remains offered a new lure to explorers willing to brave the dangers of the country.

hill. "It is nearly 800 yards in length and about 350 yards at its extreme breadth. . . . About a third of the height from its base a massive wall . . . is carried completely around the eminence and flanked by square towers. . . ." Within the entrance, raised 10 feet above a platform, he found the inscriptions. Also within the massive walls were the ruins of a temple. This was Nakab al Hajar, one of the very few walled towns of southern Arabia, which dates back to about 1000 B.C.

This expedition was the first made by Europeans into the southern interior. The results thrilled explorers and archaeologists alike. The inscriptions found at Nakab al Hajar and Husn Ghorab furnished the first decisive proof to Europeans that Himyaritic records survived from the ancient Sabaean civilizations. Greatly encouraged by his finds at these two ancient sites, Wellsted wanted to explore farther in southern Arabia and, in particular, to reach the Wadi

Above: James Theodore Bent, who openly led a scientific expedition into the Hadhramaut in 1893. He was accompanied by his wife, who took photographs of the journey.

Right: exploration in Yemen, the Hejaz, and the Hadhramaut. In the Hejaz, exploration was made more difficult by the fact that the region around the holy cities was forbidden to non-Moslems, but all over Arabia explorers encountered the fierce religious fanaticism of Islam. Many of these explorers risked their lives to bring back reports of Arabia.

Hadhramaut. But when he tried to plan other journeys, he found his way barred by the hostility of the Arab population.

The Arabs of the Hadhramaut were among the fiercest opponents of European exploration. They had always been passionately concerned with their freedom, and their fury was aroused by the British seizure of Aden in January, 1839. Furthermore, the *sayids*—Moslem holy men who believe they are descended from Mohammed through his daughter Fatima—incited the Arab townspeople to attack any explorers foolhardy enough to try to penetrate the interior. The few travelers who did manage to penetrate as far inland as Tarīm had their clothing ripped off, their maps and notes stolen, and were soon terrified into retreat. It is only comparatively recently that the sayids' complete and exclusive control over religion, law, and learning in the Hadhramaut has been broken.

The ferocity of the sayids and their followers prevented further expeditions into the interior of the Hadhramaut for nearly 60 years. Then, at the end of 1893, an Englishman, James Theodore Bent, led an undisguised expedition into the interior. Despite the fears of the British officials at Aden, who were still opposed to the idea of provoking the tribesmen, Bent and his companions set out to explore inland from Al Mukallā. The Aden government derived some comfort from the fact that Theodore Bent had among his party a surveyor and mapmaker who might bring back some useful information about the inland regions. Also in the group were an Egyptian naturalist, a botanist from the Royal Botanical Gardens in London, and Mrs. Bent, who took photographs of the expedition.

On leaving Al Mukallā, the Bents' expedition climbed slowly and steadily to about 4,000 feet. There they found themselves on the broad level tableland which isolates the Wadi Hadhramaut from the south coast. After two more days of arduous travel, they began to approach the entrances of the wadis which lead on to the Wadi Hadhramaut. At first, they met with a hostile reception from the Bedouins, but when they entered the Wadi Hadhramaut the situation began to improve.

According to Mrs. Bent, as far as Shibām "... all was desert and sand, but suddenly the valley narrows and a long vista of cultivation was spread before us. Here miles of the valley are covered with palm groves. Bright green patches of lucerne called *kadhib,* almost dazzling to look upon after the arid waste. . . ."

64

Below: a group of Hadhramaut tribesmen. This photograph was taken by
Harold Ingrams, a British government
official who, in the 1930's, managed
to bring peace to the area. Earlier
explorers had been hindered by the
constant intertribal struggles which
used to take place in the Hadhramaut.

The Bents managed to travel to Shibām despite a tribal feud in the area, but the Arabs' hostility soon forced them to leave the town. On their return, they received more insults and threats from the townspeople. In the safety of the sultan's palace, the Bents discussed their next move. They decided to make for the coast at Shihr, rather than Al Mukallā, using the Wadi Adim, a more easterly route than that by which they had come.

It was a hard and dangerous journey. The Hamumi tribe which dominated a long section of the route was involved in a war, and the Bents' party was attacked several times. When they reached the head of the wadi and emerged onto the surrounding plateau, it still proved to be difficult going. It was March, 1894, before they at last reached the safety of the coast.

Later that year, the Bents made another expedition, this time in Dhofar, farther along the southern Arabian coast toward Muscat. They found the ruins of seven ancient towns and ventured inland to the Qara Mountains. At the high point of the range, it was possible to stand looking northward into the Rub' al Khali, the Empty Quarter, and then to turn around and see the Arabian Sea. During this trip, as on their previous expeditions, the Bents collected lists of ancient words which they copied from inscriptions. They also took back samples of rare plants, shells, and insects.

Tribal quarrels had prevented the Bents from journeying along the Wadi Hadhramaut beyond Shibām to visit the ancient towns of Say'ūn and Tarīm. Nor were they able to see the tomb of the prophet Hud, or Bir Borhut, said by legend to be like a dark well or smoking volcano, where the souls of infidels could be heard moaning in agony. Forty years were to pass before these places were visited by a European.

In 1931, a Dutch Orientalist and former diplomat, Van der Meulen, and a German, Von Wissman, were sent by the Dutch government to explore the Hadhramaut. Thousands of Hadhramis had emigrated to the Dutch East Indies, where the prospects of making money were considerably better than in Arabia. This pattern of emigration had developed during World War I, and continued afterward. The Hadhramis remained in the Indies until they had made sufficient money, and then returned to spend the rest of their lives in Arabia. The Dutch government wanted to find out more about the country these immigrant workers came from.

As the Bents had done, Van der Meulen and Von Wissman started out from Al Mukallā. Although they had used an automobile for one or two local trips, when they set out to explore the Hadhramaut they traveled in the old way—on camels in the comparative safety of a caravan. The first place they visited was the Wadi Doan, which impressed them with its beauty. "The sun shines right into the wadi, where no life or movement are to be seen. Between patches of gay yellowish-green, formed by the fields of dhura, maize, and lucerne, lies unruffled the broad, shining, gray-green strip of date-groves. . . . This is the reward of weary travelers in the desert. . . . In spite of the heat, we cannot tear ourselves away from the spell cast by this valley full of fertility and beauty, in the midst of an endless desert of barren rock and stone."

Von Wissman and Van der Meulen traveled from the Wadi Doan to the Wadi Hadhramaut. The tribal quarrels which had prevented the Bents from visiting the ancient towns along the wadi were no longer an obstacle, and at both Say'ūn and Tarīm the travelers were received as honored guests. At Tarīm, the remotest and richest of the three towns of the wadi, the two men visited Sayid Abu-Bakr al-Kaf, the leading citizen of the area. Abu-Bakr had used his share of the income from the rich family fortune to build roads and schools, and to improve the living standard of the Bedouins. The explorers were greatly impressed by this man, whose name was to remain linked with the idea of a modern, peaceful Hadhramaut.

From Tarīm, Von Wissman and Van der Meulen made the two-day journey eastward to the tomb of Hud. According to the story, Hud had fled to this place pursued by his enemies. God opened the rock for him to escape, and his pursuers saw him no more. This important Moslem sanctuary was normally barred to non-Moslems,

Left: the high rocky hinterland of the Hadhramaut—the *jol*. The Bents were among the first explorers to reach this remote area of southern Arabia.

Right: Von Wissman and Van der Meulen (in the center) with Sayid Abu-Bakr al-Kaf and three of the sayid's aides. Abu-Bakr continued to work for a modern Hadhramaut until his death in 1967.

Below: the tomb of the prophet Hud, which Van der Meulen and Von Wissman visited under the protection of Abu-Bakr. According to the traditional belief, the dark rock in the picture is the petrified camel of the prophet.

but as Abu-Bakr's friends, Von Wissman and Van der Meulen were allowed to visit it. From Hud's tomb, the travelers passed through another wild and rocky wadi to visit the legendary volcano of Bir Borhut. It was something of an anticlimax. At Bir Borhut there was no volcano, and nothing to confirm the ancient legends of souls writhing in torment. Von Wissman and Van der Meulen simply found a deep cave, or series of caves, in the limestone rock, oppressively hot and eerily populated by bats.

Far left: Doreen Ingrams, who became famous to the secluded women and the children of the wadi villages. The men respected her for her endurance—she was able to ride a camel as untiringly as any of the desert patrols.

Left: Harold Ingrams. His success lay mainly in his ability to persuade the Hadhramaut people to abandon their intertribal struggles and work together for improvements in their life.

The next important explorer of the Hadhramaut was an Englishman, Harold Ingrams, who with his wife, Doreen, effectively opened up the area by establishing peace among the warring tribesmen. In the 1930's, the various states, towns, villages, and hamlets, were still constantly fighting among themselves, just as they had for over a century. When, in 1934, Ingrams was sent by the British government to be resident adviser at Al Mukallā, he set himself the task of trying to understand the people of the Hadhramaut region and their intertribal squabbles.

During the first three years of the Ingrams' stay in Al Mukallā, Doreen Ingrams worked among the women and children of the wadi villages. In this secluded region, women had for centuries been kept in complete subjugation to their husbands, and knew nothing about the world beyond their villages. Doreen Ingrams succeeded in making friends with them, and was even welcomed in the harems.

The Ingrams believed that progress could come to the region only through a long period of internal peace. The people wanted responsibility for their own way of life. In 1937, Harold Ingrams negotiated a treaty with the Sultan of Shihr and Al Mukalla. This established the idea of a resident adviser in the area, who would help organize a modern government and a scheme for constructing roads and schools. More important than this treaty, was the truce which Ingrams also arranged between the tribes—the *Sulh Ingrams,* or the Ingrams' truce—which at last brought a period of peace and

progress to the feuding, battle-weary people of the Hadhramaut.

In 1939, the Dutch explorer Van der Meulen made another trip to the Hadhramaut and was struck by the change from a land of war to one of peace. He writes: "The fortresses, the lookout towers, the trenches, all of which had been manned during our previous visit, were now deserted. Neglected gardens were irrigated again and the gates of walled villages and of fortified farm dwellings, in which men and women had lived as prisoners, were now wide open. Rifles and cartridges had lost their value and had disappeared from daily life. Women and children walked freely on roads and paths where one formerly met only men, well armed and in groups. A dying land with parched fields and date groves struggling against the sandblown wind, had put on a fresh garment of green, and with it life and happiness."

During the time they spent in the Hadhramaut, Harold and Doreen Ingrams also traveled in the inland regions which were still unknown to Europeans. They visited the Seiar Bedouins who lived in the area bordering the dreaded Rub' al Khali, and by talking to the Seiar chiefs tried to understand the way of life of this particularly wild tribe. They also ventured into the Mahra country of Tarīm. Their travels completed the exploration of the Wadi Hadhramaut, and helped to fill in the last blanks on the map of the region. When an aerial survey of the area was carried out, the exploration of the Hadhramaut was complete.

Above: three typical people of the tribes of the Hadhramaut, a photograph taken by Doreen Ingrams.

The Heart of Arabia

5

The heart of Arabia—the Nejd—was opened up to European explorers only after the Egyptian armies had heavily defeated the Wahhabis in 1818. Until this time, even the most carefully disguised traveler was in danger of being killed by the fanatical Wahhabis. For it was there, in the very middle of the Nejd, that Abd al-Wahhab, the founder of this extreme form of Islam, had been born in 1703. There the most fanatical supporters of his sect were found.

Geography as well as religious fanaticism kept the Nejd a closed area to European explorers until the mid-1800's. The traveler approaching from the north, east, or south has to cross vast stretches of sand desert before he reaches the cities and oases of this heartland of Arabia. To the west lie the Hejaz and the holy cities—a forbidden region to non-Moslem Europeans.

In the years between 1860 and 1880 a small band of explorers—most of them British—managed to penetrate this part of Arabia. Between them they investigated, described, and mapped great areas that on all earlier charts had been marked as unknown.

The first of these explorers was William Palgrave. In the summer of 1862, accompanied by a Syrian named Barakat, Palgrave crossed the An Nafūd, the desert north of the Nejd. Palgrave described it as

an immense ocean of loose reddish sand, heaped up into enormous ridges about 300 feet high. In the valleys between these great dunes, Palgrave and his companions felt imprisoned, hemmed in on all sides. Palgrave also experienced the *simoom,* the hot suffocating desert wind, when he and Barakat, accompanied by three Bedouins, were crossing the desert between Ma'ān and Wadi as Sirhan.

In his journal, Palgrave describes the first abrupt, burning gusts of wind. The horizon darkened to a deep violet. The Bedouins wrapped their cloaks around their heads and dropped to the ground to protect themselves from the burning wind and sand. Soon a stifling blast of hot air forced the camels to lie down on the sand. Everyone in the party lay covered up as much as possible for 10 minutes, while a still heat like a red-hot iron passed over them. Then came more gusts of wind, and the Bedouins unmuffled their faces. The worst was over. Palgrave and Barakat, however, both felt that their strength had been completely sapped by the heat. The camels lay flat as though dead from exhaustion. Then the sky, which had remained dark, began to grow lighter. At last it regained its dazzling clarity, the camels got up, and the small caravan remounted to resume its march across the desert.

Above: a pilgrim camp at Birkejemas-neh, sketched by Lady Anne Blunt who traveled through the Nejd with her husband between 1878 and 1879. The Nejd has often been referred to as the heart of Arabia.
Below: William Gifford Palgrave, the British traveler and author, who was the first European to enter the Nejd.

When they reached the Nejd itself, Palgrave and Barakat, both now disguised as Syrian doctors, made their way to the center. Along the route they rested at Riyadh, the capital of the Nejd. Then they traveled to Hofuf, a town near the Persian Gulf. From there they proceeded to Al Qatīf on the coast. On reaching Al Qatīf, Palgrave became the first European explorer to cross the Arabian Peninsula from west to east. It had taken eight months from Gaza, on the Mediterranean coast, to Al Qatīf, on the Persian Gulf.

Charles Montagu Doughty was among the next to venture into the Nejd. He too was an Englishman and had already traveled widely in Europe and the Middle East. In 1876, he set out from Damascus. For the first stage of the journey to the Nejd, Doughty traveled with a pilgrim caravan. But at Medā'in Sālih he left the caravan, and after four months there set out eastward into the heart of Arabia. Doughty was alone, except when he joined groups of Bedouin. He traveled slowly from place to place, spending in all two years in

Below: the An Nafūd, the vast red sand desert of Arabia, an enormous expanse of desolation lying to the north of the Nejd. It was in the An Nafūd that Palgrave encountered the burning desert wind, the *simoom*.

Arabia. He visited Taymā', Hā'il, Buraydah, and 'Unayzah. Finally he turned southwest and, skirting the holy city of Mecca, reached the Red Sea port of Juddah.

Doughty was anxious to live the life of the Arabs. He traveled as a Christian, sharing as far as he could the life of the tribesmen, experiencing the heat, hunger, and thirst, joining in the quarrels of the nomads' life. After returning exhausted to England in 1878, he worked for nearly 10 years turning his notes into *Travels in Arabia Deserta,* an important book about Arabia and the Arabs.

In 1878, just a few months after Doughty had completed his wanderings, an English couple set out on an expedition into the Nejd. Wilfrid Scawen Blunt was then 38 years of age. As a British diplomat, he had served in Athens, Madrid, Paris, and Lisbon. With his wife, Lady Ann Blunt, and a party of Bedouins, he set out from Damascus to reach the Nejd. Also in the party was a young sheik who was returning to his tribe to find himself a wife. His presence was a protection for the Blunts, who never pretended to be Moslems. The fact that they were traveling with the sheik probably also enabled them to carry instruments such as a compass and a

Above: Wilfrid Scawen Blunt, shown
mounted on his Arabian horse, Pharaoh.
Right: although the Blunts' journey
was generally peaceful, there was one
frightening incident, when they were
attacked by mounted horsemen in the
desert. They were saved only by
the intervention of a young sheik
traveling with them. This water color
by Lady Anne shows the moment before
the sheik rode up to rescue them.

barometer, and to take notes openly without provoking the Arabs.

The Blunts, like Doughty, visited the city of Hā'il in the northern Nejd. There they were received by the ruler of the region, Mohammed ibn Rashid. He seemed to respect their lack of disguise, but some of the Wahhabis in Hā'il were hostile toward the party, especially to Blunt's wife.

One of the Blunts' reasons for going to the Nejd was to buy Arab horses to take back to England for breeding. They were delighted, therefore, when Ibn Rashid showed them his stable, which was one of the most famous in Arabia. As it was winter, the horses were ungroomed, and the Blunts' first impression was very disappointing. "We made the mistake, too common, of judging horses by condition, for, mounted and in motion, these at once became transfigured," wrote Lady Anne.

The Blunts' travels through the Nejd were on the whole peaceful, perhaps because they were accompanied by the sheik. They were, however, attacked by tribesmen in Wadi Sirhan. The rest of the party had gone on ahead. The Blunts dismounted and sat on the ground to rest. Suddenly they heard the thunder of hooves and looked up to see a group of horsemen charging down on them with lances. Lady Anne had sprained her knee and could not mount her

horse fast enough to escape. The horsemen rode up to Blunt, grabbed his gun, and began to hit him over the head with it. Lady Anne pleaded that she and her husband meant no harm and would surrender. Fortunately the young sheik who was accompanying the Blunts soon arrived on the scene. The attackers recognized that he was from a friendly tribe. The danger was over and peace was restored.

On their journey through the An Nafūd to the Persian Gulf coast, the Blunts were able, as they had hoped, to buy a number of magnificent horses from the Arab tribesmen. The stud that Blunt established with these horses at his home in England is still one of the most famous in the world.

More than 30 years passed between the Blunts' journey and the next visit of a woman explorer to Hā'il. Between 1899 and 1913, Gertrude Bell had made many journeys in the Middle East, but her ambition was to travel in Arabia itself. In 1913, she achieved this aim when she became the second woman to visit Hā'il. Miss Bell wrote many books about her travels, but none of them give a full account of this Arabian journey. During her journeys, however, she gained enough knowledge of Arabia and the Middle East to be appointed to the Arab intelligence bureau during World War I.

Above: a phtograph of Lady Anne Blunt in Arab dress. Lady Anne took a vigorous part in the expedition, and kept a careful record of the sights they saw. Her exquisite water color paintings capture the barren beauty of the heart of Arabia — the Nejd.

The Empty Quarter

6

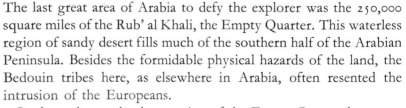

The last great area of Arabia to defy the explorer was the 250,000 square miles of the Rub' al Khali, the Empty Quarter. This waterless region of sandy desert fills much of the southern half of the Arabian Peninsula. Besides the formidable physical hazards of the land, the Bedouin tribes here, as elsewhere in Arabia, often resented the intrusion of the Europeans.

In the early 1930's, the crossing of the Empty Quarter became a race between two Englishmen—Bertram Thomas and St. John Philby. Both men had started their careers as British officials in the Middle East—Thomas in Iraq and Transjordan and Philby in Iraq. Both had later transferred to the service of Arab rulers in lands bordering on the Empty Quarter. Thomas became adviser to the Sultan of Muscat and Oman. Philby converted to Islam and became an adviser to King Abdul Aziz ibn Saud of Saudi Arabia.

By chance, both Thomas and Philby planned to cross the Empty Quarter in the winter of 1930–1931. Thomas was the first to set out. The lands of the sultan for whom he worked bordered the southeast corner of the Empty Quarter. Thomas decided to start from Dhofar, the fertile region in the west of Muscat and Oman, and cross the

Left: wind-blown sand dunes in the vast Empty Quarter of Arabia, the Rub' al Khali. Survival in the Arabian desert, even for the most experienced Bedouin, remains a test of endurance, a battle with hunger and thirst, the bitter cold at night and burning heat by day.

Right: Bertram Thomas in 1926, four years before he became the first European to cross the Rub' al Khali.

79

Above: a group of desert travelers prepare for the onslaught of a sandstorm. When the first explorers ventured into the Rub' al Khali, the desert tribesmen were still hostile to Europeans and attack was always possible. Even today, desert travelers still carry arms.

Empty Quarter from south to north with a Bedouin escort. Early in December, 1930, 40 Bedouin Rashidis arrived in Dhofar, led by Sheik Salih bin Yakut. Thomas proceeded to argue and bargain with the sheik about the terms under which the Bedouins would agree to accompany him. In due course agreement was reached, and on December 10 the expedition set out.

Thomas' route was to be first north across the mountains behind Dhofar, then westward for some distance over the firm, steppe country—a large, empty, and cool area—along the edge of the sands. He then intended to head north again, directly across the sands toward the Qatar Peninsula on the Persian Gulf, a total distance of 700 miles. As they traveled along the edge of the sands the Bedouins pointed out tracks though the dunes. These, they said, led in two days to the site of a city called Ubar, which had been swallowed up by the sand. There is no doubt, says Thomas, that the sand had encroached southward, and might have engulfed a town in such a place. He wondered if there could have been some old trade route in those parts when physical conditions were less severe. He also wondered whether "Ubar" could be the Arabs' name for Ophir,

Above right: Bertram Thomas with his Bedouin escort. He traveled with them living as they lived, dressing as they dressed, sharing the uncompromising hardships of their life in the desert.

Below: St. John Philby with his camel in Riyadh, shortly before he made his crossing of the Rub' al Khali.

according to the Bible the source of much of King Solomon's treasure of gold and jewels.

By early January Thomas' party had left the firm steppe for the exhausting, shifting sand. At the water hole of Shanna, they were inside the Empty Quarter. The Rashidi escort was on the alert for Seiar raiders from the country north of the Hadhramaut, who were reported to be in the neighbourhood. Although there were false alarms, no fighting took place. Thomas had decided on Shanna as the starting point for the most difficult part of the trip, the final 400 miles. The party for this last stretch consisted of 13 men and their camels, and 5 pack animals carrying rations for 25 days.

On January 10, 1931, Thomas and the Rashidi set out from Shanna. Two weeks later there was a severe sandstorm. Another day or two brought them to the well of Banaiyan, on the northern fringe of the Empty Quarter and little more than 80 miles from the Persian Gulf. They had covered the 270 miles from Shanna in 18 days, an average of 15 miles a day. The job was virtually done.

On February 5, they saw the towers of Doha silhouetted against the waters of the Persian Gulf. "Half an hour later," records

Above: a photograph by Philby showing his car in Wadi Luja, to the east of At Tā'if. The photographs Philby gave to the Royal Geographical Society in London were the first glimpses the outside world had of many of the remote areas of Arabia.

Right: part of Thesiger's party in the Rub' al Khali. Thesiger entered whole-heartedly into the life of his Bedouin companions, even going barefoot as they did. He was the last of the old-fashioned explorers of the deserts of Arabia.

Above: an Arabian coffeepot. Even in the desert, the serving and drinking of coffee remain a ritual for the Arabs.

Below: Philby's desert coffee mill and roaster. The coffee was roasted in the ladle over the open campfire.

Thomas, "we entered the walls of the fort. The Rub' al Khali had been crossed." It was a remarkable achievement. Only two years earlier a man who knew the Arabian deserts well—the Englishman T. E. Lawrence, "Lawrence of Arabia"—had written of the Empty Quarter that "only an airship could cross it."

Only chance prevented St. John Philby from attacking the Empty Quarter from the northern side during that same winter of 1930–1931. To his disappointment, the Saudi Arabian government refused him vacation to make the crossing. Instead, he heard of Thomas' success when he was on the point of starting nearly a year later. But although Philby could not now be the first, his achievement is in many ways as great as that of Thomas. Thomas was first, and made the journey at his own cost. He traveled as a Christian and his journey was well planned. Philby, on the other hand, did not do enough planning. He had the advantage of being a Moslem, and of having the backing of the powerful Saudi king. But he also spent longer in the Empty Quarter and made a more sensational crossing.

Philby's party set out from Hofuf on January 7, 1931. They traveled southeast toward the Qatar Peninsula and then southwest across the Al Jāfūrah desert to the Jabrin Oasis. From there, they followed a zigzag course that brought them onto Thomas' route at roughly the halfway point through the sands. Philby then went southward to the Shanna water hole from which Thomas' party had started out. Then, having almost completed the crossing from north to south, Philby decided to go westward from Shanna through the Empty Quarter. His target was As Sulayyil, nearly 400 miles away, at the southernmost point of the great Tuwayq mountain range.

This first attempt on "the veritable desert," as Philby calls it, nearly ended in disaster. The party made the mistake of taking heavily laden pack animals with them. When they were just over 100 miles from Shanna, and the same distance away from any other water, even the hardy camels began to suffer from heat and exhaustion. The expedition had to turn back, making for Naifa, north of Shanna and almost on Thomas' route. This first thrust westward

MEDITERRANEAN
SEA

Euphrates

Damascus

Tigris

Baghdad

Euphrates

Petra

An Nafud

PERSIAN GULF

Taymāʾ

Medāʾin Sālih

Haʾil

Hofuf

Qatar
Pena.
Doha

Ash Shāriqah

GULF OF OM

Buraydah
Unayzah

Al Jafūrah

Abū Ẓaby

TROPIC OF CANCER

Riyadh

Jabrin

Banaiyan

Liwa
Oasis

TROPIC OF

Juddah
Mecca

As Sulayyil

Naifa

Mughshin

R u b ʿ   a l   K h a l i

Dhofār

Shanna

Manwakh

Hadhramaut

Al Mukallā

RED   SEA

GULF OF ADEN

INDIA

OCEAN

© Geographical Projects

0   100   200   300   400

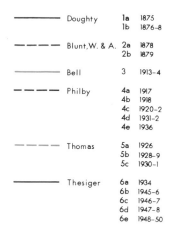

———	Doughty	1a	1875
		1b	1876–8
– – –	Blunt, W. & A.	2a	1878
		2b	1879
———	Bell	3	1913–4
– – –	Philby	4a	1917
		4b	1918
		4c	1920–2
		4d	1931–2
		4e	1936
– – –	Thomas	5a	1926
		5b	1928–9
		5c	1930–1
———	Thesiger	6a	1934
		6b	1945–6
		6c	1946–7
		6d	1947–8
		6e	1948–50

Below: a swarm of locusts filling
the sky. These voracious insects
descend in their millions, completely destroying crops. Thesiger
first became interested in the Rub'
al Khali when he visited Arabia to
investigate locust breeding grounds.
Below right: a single locust. Locusts
eat green leaves and stalks and,
because they travel in such huge
numbers, a swarm can destroy the
vegetation over a large area.

and the subsequent retreat made two long sides of a triangle with
Philby's route to Shanna as the base. From Naifa, in the first days of
March, Philby led a smaller, more mobile party to make a second
strike westward. The party reached As Sulayyil on March 15. It was
a desperate effort—"375 miles or more between water and water,"
says Philby—and it tested men and animals to the utmost. Over 6
successive days, 3 of them very hot, they had kept up an average of
40 miles a day. One march lasted 21 hours, including rest periods
totaling 3 hours, and covered 70 miles. Small wonder that Philby
later remarked that crossing the Empty Quarter was "an adventure
not to be lightly undertaken by the uninitiated."

Like Thomas, with his interest in the buried city of Ubar, Philby
became fascinated by tales of a legendary city called Wabar that was
reported to be hidden somewhere in the Empty Quarter. Many
years before, Bedouin tribesmen had told him about a city which
had been destroyed by fire because its wicked ruler would not heed
the warnings of the prophet Hud. The story stuck in Philby's mind.
When he and his party eventually reached the supposed site, however, they found no ruined city. All that Philby could find were two
huge craters caused by meteorites.

Thomas and Philby both crossed the Empty Quarter in the early
1930's. By that time, many people thought that the day of the old-
fashioned Arabian explorer, depending for his mobility on his
animals and his own feet, had gone. But one more of the same type
did appear in Arabia—a man of the highest ability by any standards.
This was Wilfred Thesiger, an Englishman whose crossings of the
Empty Quarter are only a small part of his great achievements as
explorer and traveler.

Thesiger was born in 1910 in Addis Ababa, capital of Ethiopia,
where his father was the British minister. The event took place,
he says, in "one of the mud huts which in those days housed the
Legation." Thesiger continued all his life to prefer mud huts to the
conventional dwellings of European civilization. By serving as a
government official in the Sudan in the 1930's and a soldier in the
Middle East during World War II, he became thoroughly familiar
with the desert and its people. After the war he volunteered for
further service in Arabia, this time joining a group whose aim was
to control the spread of locusts in the desert. Experts believed that

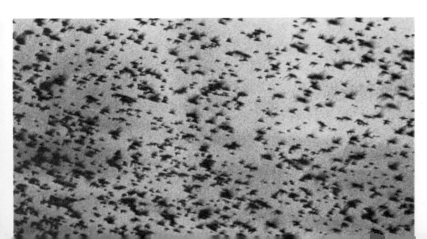

these grasshopper-like insects that descend in swarms upon vegetation, devouring every scrap, bred in areas north of Dhofar. It was while investigating these breeding grounds that Thesiger, like Thomas and Philby before him, became fascinated by the challenge of the Empty Quarter.

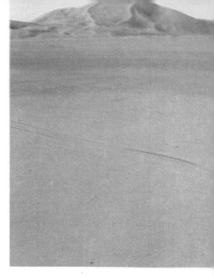

Thesiger crossed the Empty Quarter twice. The first time he took with him an escort of four Rashidi, members of the same tribe Thomas had found so cooperative. The small party crossed from Mughshin, north of Dhofar, to the Liwa Oasis, not far from Abū Zaby on the Persian Gulf. This route lay well to the east of that taken by Thomas more than 10 years before. On the return journey, Thesiger skirted the sands by traveling in a semicircle through the gravel desert of Oman.

In 1947, Thesiger decided to complete the exploration of the Empty Quarter by investigating the western sands. He set out across the desert from the well of Manwakh in the far north of the Hadhramaut country, aiming for the town of As Sulayyil nearly 400 miles north. It took Thesiger 16 days to make the journey across a completely waterless stretch of desert. There was constant fear of attack from tribesmen who were still, even in the 1940's, hostile to travelers from outside. When at last Thesiger and his companions reached As Sulayyil, they were arrested by the Saudi authorities. The precise reason for their arrest was never made clear to them. Only after Philby, at that time still an official of the Saudi Arabian government, had used his influence with the king were they finally released. From As Sulayyil, Thesiger traveled east, through Jabrin to the Trucial States.

While Thesiger was traveling in the Empty Quarter, a new kind of explorer was moving into Arabia. In 1942, in the middle of World War II, the United States government, in cooperation with the King of Saudi Arabia, sent an expedition to the Hejaz, the Nejd, and Yemen. Its aim was to investigate the natural resources of the desert. When World War II ended in 1945, foreign technicians, agricultural experts, and geologists flooded into Arabia. The most fateful discovery had, however, been made some years before.

In 1932, oil was first discovered in Bahrain. Shortly afterward, the Arabian American Oil Company was formed to survey vast areas in the eastern coastal region along the Persian Gulf. They, too, were soon successful, and the oil they found brought unexpected wealth to this otherwise poor region. Further important finds were made under the waters of the Persian Gulf in 1951, 1958, and 1960. By 1970, the Arabian American Oil Company alone was paying Saudi Arabia $500 million a year for its oil.

The discovery and exploitation of the oil and the subsequent introduction of modern technology soon changed the life of the Bedouins. Thesiger stayed in Arabia for a few more years, but life became increasingly difficult for the old-fashioned explorer investigating the desert for its own sake. The Saudis, traditionally suspicious, denounced him as a spy in radio broadcasts. "Few people,"

Thesiger wrote, "accepted the fact that I traveled there for my own pleasure, certainly not the American oil companies or the Saudi government." He saw too that the Bedouin way of life was changing The nomadic Bedouins were signing on as unskilled laborers in the oil fields. When Thesiger said good-by to the two Bedouins who had been his companions since he first came to Arabia, they rode away, not on camels, but perched on gasoline drums on the back of a truck. Thesiger himself was driven to the airfield at Ash Shāriqah on the Persian Gulf, and flew out. The year was 1950. The last great phase of Arabian exploration was over.

Left: a truck drives across the desert. Today, mechanized transportation is replacing the camel and is irrevocably altering the life of the Bedouin.

Below: a desert oil rig. The discovery of oil has brought wealth to Arabia.

The Vast Sahara 7

Like the Arabian Peninsula, the arid wastes of the Sahara desert long fascinated the peoples of Europe. Explorers were attracted by the challenge of the hostile climate and the difficult terrain. Merchants wanted to share in the trade on caravan routes over the Sahara. Historians and scholars were interested in the relics of the past. But there was another pressing reason for the Europeans' interest in the Sahara. It lay between Europe and the great river that Europeans called the Niger—the *black river*. Although in the 1700's Europeans knew of the existence of the river, no one had yet charted its course. Many of the adventurers who set out to explore the Niger

believed the best way to reach the river was to travel south over the vast, burning expanse of the Sahara.

Most people think of the Sahara as an unending sea of sand. In the west, this is true enough. The dune areas—called *ergs,* from an Arabic word—are vast. In Algeria, the Grand Erg Occidental and the Grand Erg Oriental each covers 20,000 square miles. But these sandy regions make up only one third of the whole Sahara area. Elsewhere are gravelly wastes, huge plains of stones and boulders, and high mountain ranges such as the Ahaggar, the Tassili-n-Ajjer, the Aïr, and the Tibesti. Scattered across this barren land are the

Above: part of the almost endless expanse of sandy waste that forms much of the Sahara – this area is near the oasis of Siwah, on the old route of the Cairo-Marzūq caravan.

Above: a Tuareg, one of the veiled men of the desert. The Tuareg people — proud and often hostile to outsiders — are nomadic tribesmen who used to control the routes across the Sahara.

Right: the Souf oasis in the Algerian Sahara. Oases are places in the desert where there is water. The water usually comes from springs, which are fed from water underground. Today, wells have been dug at many oases, and the surrounding land irrigated so that crops can be grown.

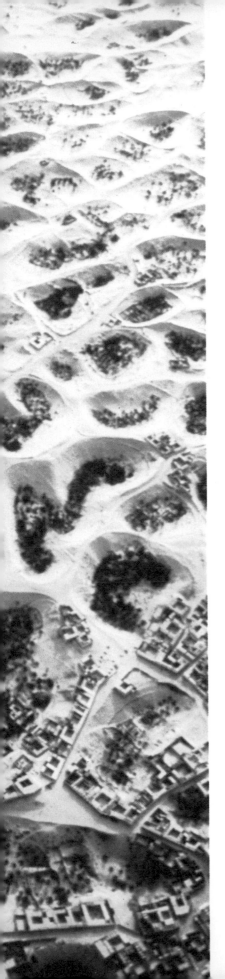

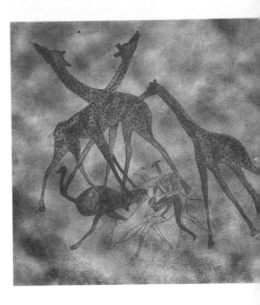

Right: the Sahara was probably not always as arid as it is today. There is evidence that plants and animals that could no longer survive in the barren land flourished there comparatively recently. This desert rock painting of about 3500 B.C. shows men hunting giraffes and an ostrich.

life-supporting oases. These isolated green patches cover only some 780 square miles—that is, less than 3 per cent of the entire area of the Sahara.

South of the Aïr and Tibesti mountains lies the great geographical region known as the Sudan. This, too, is usually considered as part of the Sahara. Stretching right across Africa, the Sudan forms a broad transitional belt between the dry desert to the north and the rain forests of equatorial Africa to the south. It is an area of savanna grasslands, with vegetation ranging from scrub and small desert plants in the north to tall grass interspersed with trees farther south. And through the west of the Sudan flows the Niger River. To get there, however, the explorers first had to conquer the hostile Sahara and its still more hostile tribesmen.

The total population of the Sahara evens out at less than one person for every square mile. Much of the desert is, however, completely uninhabited, save for the wandering tribesmen, while in the oases overpopulation is common. Only some two-thirds of the people of the oasis townships live there all the time. The rest of the population is constantly changing, as the nomadic groups wander from place to place. The peoples of the northern desert are Arabs and Berbers, while in the extreme south live Negro tribesmen, and in the southeast the Tibbu people, Negroes of mixed ancestry. The desert nomads are mainly Berbers, and in the Ahaggar and Tassili-n-Ajjer mountain regions they are called *Tuareg*. It is the Tuareg who for centuries have controlled the oasis settlements and the caravan routes between them. It was the Tuareg who frequently determined the success or failure of European expeditions.

The vegetation of the Sahara, however varied it may appear, has two common characteristics. First, it can withstand long dry periods. Second, it is able to race through life processes when water is available. This is particularly necessary in the Sahara, where rain falls only infrequently. In a year, an average of four inches of rain falls

Above: Algerian street sellers squat on the ground, surrounded by their heaped piles of dates. The best dates reportedly come from Jarbah, a small island off Tunisia.

on the Sahara. The rainfall is not, however, spread evenly over the year, but occurs in occasional torrential downpours. When rain falls, it quickly seeps through the parched surface to the subterranean deposits of water from which many of the oases in the sahara draw their reserves.

Although the Sahara is often thought of simply as a hot region, temperatures there do in fact vary widely. On a winter night the temperature may drop to freezing point, while in the heat of a summer day it can reach 130°F. In 24 hours the temperature can change by as much as 60° or 70°. To withstand the brutal changes of weather, man must be hardy and properly clothed. A nomad's robes of thick cloth are ideal, because they insulate him from extremes of both heat and cold.

More frequent than rain in the Sahara are sandstorms, which often have disastrous effects on vegetation, animals, and people. Sandstorms occur when the hot air above the sand rises and is replaced by colder air. A fierce wind results, which can be either constant or intermittent and turbulent. The wind picks up the sand and carries it like a large trembling net over the ground. The sun is hidden, and a wall of sand blots out the horizon. At this point it becomes impossible to see and difficult to stand upright. A sandstorm usually dies down at sunset, but it may start again the following morning, and repeat this cycle over several days.

The Sahara as a whole produces a rich variety of cultivated fruits and vegetables, but these are unevenly distributed because of variations in climate and soil. Tropical fruits and even grain are grown where irrigation has been carried out near oases, but neither ever becomes a regular cash crop. The only really valuable fruit grown in the desert is the date. Except at altitudes of over 4,500 feet, in the southern half of the desert, and along the Atlantic coast, the date palm tree supplies the basic food of the desert people. It also provides valuable exports.

Above: traces of the Roman past exist in many parts of North Africa. The Romans settled mainly in the more inviting coastal areas, but a number of military expeditions did venture into parts of the Sahara itself.

Left: the inscription of King Djer, who ruled Egypt about 3000 B.C. The inscription tells of an expedition into the Sahara, which conquered a local ruler. It is the earliest known reference to the Sahara.

In the southern part of the Sahara, the date becomes a luxury. Salt-mining is the livelihood of the people there, and salt is the chief export. Today the principal salt deposits are at Tisempt, Djado, and Taoudenni. During the Middle Ages, salt mined from these deposits was traded to merchants for gold. Today, it is still one of the desert's most important resources.

As in Arabia, life in the Sahara is largely dependent upon the camel. Even 50 years ago, the camel was still the only safe means of crossing the desert, and it has naturally played an important part in the story of exploration. Along some stretches of the Sahara caravan routes there are no wells for more than 300 miles. Only the camel enabled explorers to cross these waterless wastes.

Also like Arabia, the Sahara has never been completely unknown, or culturally stagnant. Seven thousand years ago it was probably

not a desert at all. The people of the area knew the arts of farming and of domesticating animals. In about 2000 B.C. the climate became drier, and the farmers were forced to move south. Even at that time, however, the desert was crossed by commercial caravans.

Since the time of the Roman Empire the people of the western Sahara have been in almost constant touch commercially with southern Europe and the Middle East. With the coming of the traders, the influence of European ideas and culture began to penetrate the Sahara. The Roman settlement at Ghirza (175 miles southeast of Tripoli) consisted of large fortified farms, which must have employed local Saharans as laborers and so passed on some elements of Roman life. But although a few Roman military expeditions did venture into the interior of the Sahara, the Romans seem to have been principally concerned with the Mediterranean coastal areas of Africa.

Far more widespread than the influence of Rome was the influence of the Islamic religion. In A.D. 642, the Arabs invaded northern Africa. The northern African coastlands became part of the Moslem Empire, and Islam the predominant religion of their people. As time passed, Arab Moslem traders traveled ever more frequently over the Sahara caravan routes. They spread Islam throughout western Africa, and Arabic became the common language of the area.

By the Middle Ages merchants went regularly back and forth across the Sahara to trade. Ibn-Batuta provides evidence of this. He set out in 1349 from Tangier, and crossed the western Sahara to Silla. On his return journey he traveled with a commercial caravan. In Ibn-Batuta's time, the caravan trade across the Sahara was a rich one. Sugar, brassware, books, and horses were transported south

Below: Ptolemy's map of North Africa. Ptolemy lived in the A.D. 100's, in Alexandria in Egypt. His map is most accurate in depicting the coastal areas well known to the classical world. Farther south and inland the map is either speculative or blank.

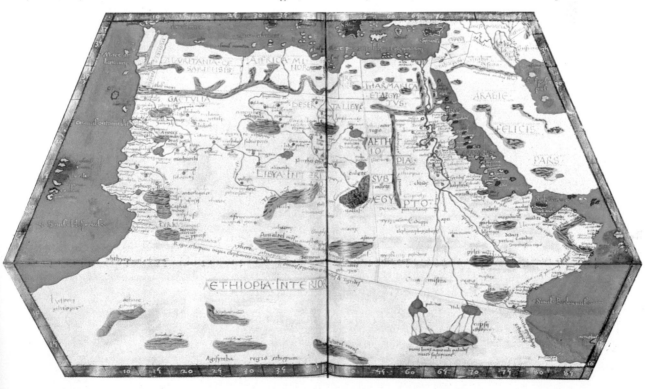

Above: el-Qara oasis, a small cluster of mud houses in the desert. It was originally founded by runaway slaves who escaped from one of the Cairo-Marzūq caravans. Slaves were one of the greatest riches of the African continent, and the slave trade there had a brutal history.

across the desert to the cities of Timbuktu and Goa. Export goods such as dates, gold, ivory, and ostrich feathers were sent north to be shipped to the kings and princes of Europe.

In the 1400's a new treasure made its first appearance in the north-bound camel caravans—slaves. Portuguese sea traders first brought slaves to sell in Europe in the mid-1400's, and slave caravans were soon making regular journeys north from Timbuktu to Fez, Tunis, and Cairo. After the discovery of the Americas, the slave trade began to take on a much greater importance. The Negroes were accustomed to tropical climate and disease, and could therefore live and work in the Caribbean area. Instead of traveling north, many slave caravans now worked their way westward to the coast, and the ports of embarkation for the Americas.

The new market for African slaves in the Americas meant a new pattern of trade in the Sahara. Shortly afterward, the Moroccans

captured the salt trade of the southwestern desert and the commercial centers along the Niger, and European interest began to shift away from the southern Sahara. But stories which had reached Europe in the 1500's of the vast wealth of Timbuktu and the other Niger cities still persisted. They were to prove an added incentive for travelers to visit these cities when Europeans began to take an interest in African exploration in the late 1700's.

The eastern Sahara, however, presents quite a different picture. Following the collapse of Roman power in Africa, the area became almost completely isolated from outside influence and trade. It was not until the 1700's that trade once again became important there, and even then it grew up only slowly.

By the 1800's, trade in the area was well under way. Caravans traveling southward through Fezzan, Cyrenaica (today part of Libya), and Egypt carried such items as cloth, rugs, sheet tin, iron and steel tools, needles, firearms, and gunpowder. Luxury goods, too, were transported across the desert to the sultans of the Sudan kingdoms. These included silks, silver and gold thread, embroidered cloth, gold and silver jewelry, mirrors, sugar, and perfumes. In the eastern Sahara, as in the west, slaves were the most important and valuable of the goods carried north across the desert. Others included ivory, gold, cotton cloth, leather goods, pepper, honey, and even live parrots.

Right: a slave caravan, drawn by George Lyon. In 1818 and 1819, Lyon traveled south from Tripoli with an expedition to find out more about the course of the Niger River. He saw several slave caravans, one consisting of 1,400 slaves of all ages.

Above: Tuareg tribesmen gathered
around the light of their campfire.
With the arrival of the Europeans
in the Sahara, the tribesmen's hold
on the caravan routes was broken.
But Tuareg raiding parties still roam
over the vast Sahara.
Below: Tuareg bodyguard of the Sheik
of Bornu, drawn by Denham in 1826.

For centuries the success of Saharan trade was at the mercy of
the warlike nomadic tribesmen who controlled the territories
through which the caravans passed. Of the many Saharan peoples,
the Tuareg are the most important. They have adopted the Moslem
religion but preserved their own language. The Tuareg are the
legendary veiled men, some of whom consider themselves to be the
aristocrats of the desert.

When the European explorers first looked toward the Sahara in
the late 1700's, the eastern caravan route from Ghāt northward
through Fezzan was controlled by the Ajjer Tuareg confederation.
The central Saharan route from In Salah southward was in the
hands of the Ahaggar tribesmen. The western caravan route seems
to have been periodically under Tuareg control, although at various
times it was ruled by other tribes and by the Moors (the Moslem
Arabic-speaking peoples of northwestern Africa). The country
around Timbuktu and the Niger bend was almost constantly
dominated by the Tuareg of the southwest.

The Tuareg based their method of controlling commercial
caravans and exploring parties on a system of furnishing armed
escorts to the groups which had to pass through areas under Tuareg
domination. For these services, they charged a fee calculated either
on the estimated value of the cargo or the reputed wealth of the
travelers who needed to be protected and directed along the route.
When caravans refused to pay the money demanded, or brought

their own guides and armed guards, the Tuareg would harass the caravans by raiding or by killing the travelers.

During the European exploration of the Sahara, the Tuareg felt increasingly threatened by the prospect of outside control. They saw the possibility of European domination as threatening their very existence, and they became increasingly hostile to explorers. The Tuareg tribal concept of an "eye for an eye" in settling disputes extended to their dealings with Europeans. And they used the Moslem religion as a convenient excuse for resisting and often murdering Christian travelers.

The conquest of the African continent held the same fascination for the Europeans of the 1800's as the exploration of space did for Americans and Russians in the 1960's. And despite the rigors of the desert climate and the ferocious Tuareg tribesmen, the exploration of the Sahara became a passion for many adventurers. Scientists, geographers, politicians, soldiers, and merchants from Europe—and in particular from Britain and France—were eager to learn about the Niger region. They believed that this mysterious area would lead them on to an even more fabulous land in the African interior. Above all, they still believed the stories which had been handed down about the huge wealth of Timbuktu and the other Niger cities. To reach this legendary treasure house they had to cross the Sahara or sail up the Niger River. But at the dawn of the 1800's no one yet knew where the mouth of the Niger lay.

Below: caravan routes in the Sahara and the Sudan. As in Arabia, caravans in the Sahara followed routes across the desert which had been used from time immemorial. The routes led across the burning sands from one oasis or water hole to the next. The distance between water and water could be several hundred miles, and the terrible journeys between taxed men and animals to the utmost.

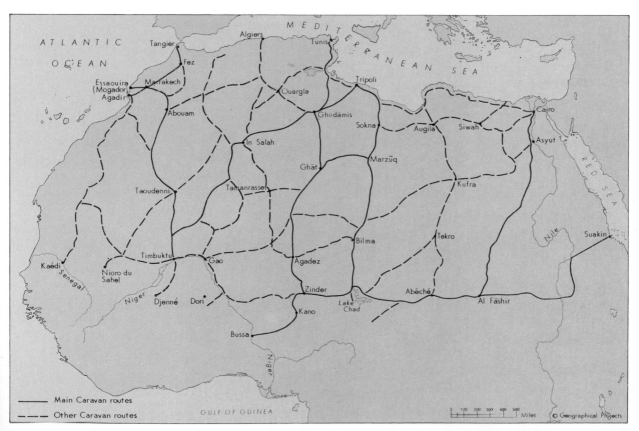

99

The African Association

8

The systematic exploration of the Sahara and the area around the Niger River began in 1788 with the formation in London of the Association for Promoting the Discovery of the Interior Parts of Africa. Sir Joseph Banks, who had explored the Pacific with Captain Cook and was the most famous British scientist of that period, founded the association. It first directed its attention to the scientific exploration of the mysterious Niger River.

At that time, little was known about the interior of Africa. No one knew for certain where the Niger River rose, in which direction it flowed, and in particular where it emptied into the sea. No one in Europe connected this river with the great delta in the Gulf of Guinea which had been known to Europeans for more than 300 years. Some people even believed that the Niger—which does in fact flow eastward in its upper reaches—flowed right across Africa to join the Nile. Others thought it might empty itself into a vast inland lake.

Banks and his colleagues quickly recruited explorers. In the same year that the association was founded, the members agreed to back an American, John Ledyard, in a journey to Timbuktu. Ledyard was an adventurer who had sailed with Captain Cook on his final

Above: a miniature portrait of Mungo Park (1771–1806). He was the third man the African Association recruited to explore Africa. His assignment was to find the source of the Niger, and to discover the river's mouth.

voyage in the Pacific. He responded enthusiastically to the association's challenging assignment to cross the Sahara from Egypt to Timbuktu. He set out almost immediately for Cairo to find a caravan that would take him across the desert. But in Cairo Ledyard fell ill with dysentery and died.

In spite of this initial failure, the African Association determined to continue their program of exploration. During this period there was much speculation about the great wealth of the trading cities in the Niger region and in particular of Timbuktu. Two Moslems who claimed that they had visited Timbuktu described its fantastic wealth and flourishing trade to the African Association. Their story confirmed the British in their belief that both the Niger and Timbuktu should be explored.

Daniel Houghton was the next man commissioned to find Timbuktu. He was an impoverished officer in the British Army who in 1790 answered the African Association's advertisement for someone to journey to "the Cities of Houssa and Tombouctoo." Houghton landed at the entrance to the Gambia River and set out east, thinking that he would be able to get safely to Timbuktu in about a month. He sent one letter home to his wife in England from the Gambia River, and a short note to the African Association in

Left: a West African village, shown in an engraving taken from a sketch by Mungo Park. The village is the typical cluster of round huts which Park must have seen many times as he traveled deep into the interior. The figure with the little goatee beard was added by the engraver, probably to represent Mungo Park himself.

Above: a pocket sextant of about 1800, probably similar to the one Park took along to determine his position in the unmapped interior.

London. But that was the last news ever heard of him.

In London, the association was eager to find a successor to Houghton. Finally, in 1794, a suitable candidate offered his services. He was Mungo Park, a 23-year-old Scottish surgeon, who had a passion for natural history. After qualifying as a doctor at Edinburgh University, Park had taken a job as a surgeon on an East India Company ship. This enabled him to pursue his hobby in the tropical waters of the Indian and Pacific oceans. In the waters around Sumatra, Park discovered and studied a new species of fish, and when he returned to London he published his description of the fish in a scientific journal. The article brought Park to the attention of Sir Joseph Banks and the African Association.

The association proposed that Park should explore the Niger River to find out where it rose and whether it flowed into the sea or some large lake. He accepted the offer at once and sailed from Portsmouth, England, in May, 1795, arriving at Pisania on the Gambia River in July. Pisania was a small village established by the British as a trading post. It was inhabited solely by British merchants and their Negro slaves. There, Park settled down to learn the Mandingo language and to collect as much information as possible about the regions he was to visit.

Right: three men silhouetted against the Bornu horizon, recalling the little group of Park, his servant Johnson, and the slave boy riding off into completely unknown territory.

Toward the end of July, Park came down with fever and delirium which confined him to his home during most of August. Subsequent bouts of the fever continued to beset him. But early in December, 1795, he set out for the interior of Africa. With him went a Negro servant named Johnson, who acted as interpreter, and a slave boy who was Park's personal servant. For the first few days of the journey the three travelers were accompanied by some slave merchants, a Negro returning to his home inland, and several other domestic slaves. Then they left the company of the merchants and slaves and set off on their own. Park rode a horse, while Johnson and the slave boy rode donkeys. They carried food for two days, beads and tobacco for bartering, a compass and pocket sextant, a thermometer, some firearms, and an umbrella. Their route was to be northeastward from the Gambia River across the Senegal River, then eastward toward Timbuktu.

After three days, Park met a local king who told him that he

Below: the bridge over the Bafing River, taken from a sketch by Park. Park began his journey in Gambia, and traveled east, crossing the Bafing River. He finally reached the Niger at Ségou, after spending three months in prison at Benown.

should go no farther. Tribesmen of the interior had never seen a white man before and would certainly kill him. But Park paid no attention to the warnings and continued eastward, traveling at night for safety. Despite all his precautions, however, he was robbed of many of his possessions during this period. When he reached Mali, which was Moslem country, the slave boy refused to go any farther. Park and Johnson started alone into the unknown and hostile interior. It was at this point that Park passed through the village of Simbing where, according to a story told by Johnson, a party of Moors—in his journal Park used the term *Moors* to describe all non-Negro Moslems—had robbed Daniel Houghton of all his possessions and perhaps killed him. Park was shown the place in the bush where Houghton's body had been thrown and left to rot.

It was not long before Park himself encountered the Moors. After some days, he was captured by a party of horsemen and taken to their headquarters at Benown, on the edge of the desert. For three months he was detained by them in very unpleasant conditions. "Never did any period of my life pass away so heavily; from sunrise to sunset I was obliged to suffer, with an unruffled countenance, the insults of the rudest savages on earth!"

Throughout this ordeal, however, Park maintained his determination to find the Niger River. He resolved to escape from the Moors, but to his disappointment Johnson was not prepared to go with him. The Negro wanted to return to his wife and family. Park recorded his feelings at the time: "Having no hopes therefore of persuading him to accompany me, I resolved to proceed by myself.

Below: the Niger River, from which the modern state of Nigeria takes its name. In the early 1800's, expedition after expedition set off into the African interior to try to solve the problem of the source and mouth of the River Niger.

Above: the early explorers of Africa found the strangeness of everything they saw one of the most disconcerting aspects of their travels. Here, Mungo Park is startled by the sight of a lion lurking in the undergrowth.

About midnight I got my clothes in readiness, which consisted of two shirts, two pair of trousers, two pocket handkerchiefs, an upper and under waistcoat, a hat, and a pair of half boots: these, with a cloak, constituted my whole wardrobe. And I had not one single bead, nor any other article of value in my possession, to purchase victuals for myself, or corn for my horse." That same night, Park managed to slip away from the hut where he had been imprisoned.

When Park had got safely away from the Moors, he journeyed into the forest to avoid being noticed. But his progress was slow because his horse, which had also been badly treated by the Moors, was in very poor condition.

Starvation and death from thirst became real possibilities, but as Park resigned himself to his end, there was a sudden thunderstorm. It continued long enough for him to spread out his clean clothes to catch the rain water and then quench his thirst by wringing and

Right: on his return journey from Silla on the banks of the Niger, Park was set upon by thieves who robbed him of all his possessions except the clothes he was wearing and his hat, in which, fortunately, he was carrying his irreplaceable notes.

sucking them. A few hours later he managed to beg a bowl of *kouskous* (a dish made from flour) from a woman who lived in one of a group of huts in the forest.

About three weeks after his escape from the Moors, Park joined a party of refugees. They assured him that he was getting near the Niger River and the great market town of Ségou. On July 20, 1796, nearly eight months after leaving the Gambia, Park had his first glimpse of the Niger at Ségou. He wrote: "I saw with infinite pleasure the great object of my mission—the long sought for majestic Niger, glittering in the morning sun, as broad as the Thames at Westminster, and flowing slowly *to the eastward*. I hastened to the brink and, having drunk of the water, lifted up my fervent thanks in prayer to the Great Ruler of all things for having thus far crowned my endeavours with success."

The fact that the Niger flowed eastward confirmed the reports Park had gathered along the way. He had made frequent inquiries about the river's direction from Negroes he had met, and they had all assured him that it flowed toward the rising sun.

Park waited for several days at Ségou in the hope of being able to visit the ruler of the area, King Mansong of Bambara. King Mansong was unwilling to receive the explorer, but eventually he sent Park a gift of money to enable him to buy provisions in the course of his journey. It seems as if this gift was meant primarily to speed the Scotsman on his way out of the kingdom.

Leaving Ségou, Park rode along the banks of the Niger for six days until he reached the town of Silla. There he realized that he could travel no farther down the river. The money which Mansong had given him was beginning to run out, but, more serious still, Park was too worn out and sick to go farther. Also, after his experience at Benown, Park was afraid of the Moors.

At the end of July, 1796, he began his return journey. After almost a month of uneventful travel, he was attacked by some robbers who took all his possessions except his trousers, his shirt, and his hat, in the crown of which he had hidden his notes. Then, in September, Park fell seriously ill with malaria at Kamalia. He was treated with kindness by a Negro slave dealer, and remained there for seven months before he set off with a slave caravan for Pisania. The caravan reached the trading post on June 10, 1797, almost 11 months after Park had first seen the Niger River.

Below: a view from the north edge of Qattara Depression, looking to the southwest. Caravans traveling from Cairo across the desert used to cross the depression and Frederick Hornemann would have followed this route to Siwah.

Above: the western end of Siwah Oasis. In ancient times, Siwah was the seat of the oracle of Zeus-Ammon. Alexander the Great visited the oracle when he was in Egypt, to consult it about his plans to conquer the Persian Empire.

Just before Christmas, 1797, Park arrived back in England. The publication of his account of his journeys two years later made him a famous man. Soon after, he returned to Scotland, where he married and set up in practice as a doctor.

In June, 1796, when Park had been a prisoner of the Moors and had not yet seen the Niger, another explorer had presented his proposed itinerary to the African Association for their approval. This man was a theological student from the University of Göttingen named Frederick Hornemann. Hornemann's plan was to join a caravan in Cairo for the Marzūq Oasis and then travel south to Katsina, a commercial and caravan center similar to Timbuktu. In order to prepare himself for the journey he spent a year learning Arabic. Then, on his way to Egypt, he passed through Paris where he received letters of introduction to Moslem merchants in Cairo, whose caravans made the desert crossing. In the autumn of 1797, Hornemann sailed from Marseille to Egypt.

In Cairo, Hornemann received a letter from Sir Joseph Banks reporting Park's safe return to the Gambia River after his journey to the Niger. Banks explained that Park had "penetrated till within

14 days of Tombouctoo, and might have enter'd that Town could he have pass'd for a Mahometan; but he desisted from the attempt on being told by all the persons he met that the Mahometans, who have the Rule of the Town, would certainly put him to death as a Christian, if he entered it. . . ." Banks's letter doubtless confirmed Hornemann's decision to travel as a Moslem. In Cairo he had met a German convert to Islam named Frendenburgh, who agreed to be his servant on the journey to Katsina. Frederick Hornemann was the first of the modern Sahara travelers to pose as a Moslem. Just as Di Varthema centuries earlier had joined a Mameluke regiment in

Above: remains of the stonework of the Temple of Zeus-Ammon at Siwah Oasis. It was Hornemann's interest in this temple which aroused the suspicion of his traveling companions that he was not, as he claimed, a Mameluke.

order to make the journey to Mecca, Hornemann claimed to be a member of a Mameluke family to help explain his fair complexion and imperfect Arabic.

Hornemann left Cairo with the caravan of 1798. It included merchants, and pilgrims who were returning from the hajj. The first important stopping place was the oasis of Siwah, where Hornemann was the second European visitor after Alexander the Great. (The first had been an Englishman, William Browne, who had visited Siwah in 1792 while exploring the western Egyptian desert.) At Siwah, Hornemann showed too obvious an interest in the remains of the Temple of Zeus-Ammon, and was accused of being non-Moslem. Some days later a party of Moslems from Siwah followed the caravan in order to challenge Hornemann's belief in Islam. They questioned him again, but the German gave a convincing enough display of his sincerity to be allowed to continue with the caravan. The route took them through the Fezzan oases at Temissa, and they reached Marzūq on November 17, 1798, about 2½ months after leaving Cairo. The distance, in a direct line, is around 1,100 miles. At Marzūq, the Sultan of Fezzan formally received the merchants and pilgrims.

Hornemann spent seven months in and around Marzūq, traveling to Tripoli to send off his reports, meeting people from many of the Saharan tribes and doubtless accumulating much information about life and travel in the desert. But journeys in the desert in the late 1700's inevitably meant disease, and in Marzūq Frendenburgh died of fever and Hornemann himself became very ill. He probably had malaria, although at that time the explorers did not always know from what form of "fever" they suffered.

By early 1800, Hornemann must have been well enough to continue his travels, and on April 6 he wrote his last letter to the African Association saying that he was about to join the Bornu caravan. At Bornu he intended to join the regular caravan to Katsina, and from there he would somehow travel southward to the coast of the Gulf of Guinea. But the association never heard from him again.

When later explorers followed Hornemann's projected route they established that he had indeed crossed the Sahara to Bornu, then traveled westward to Katsina, and south again toward the Niger. Sometime early in 1801 this courageous German had died a lonely death in an obscure village called Bokani, only a day's journey short of the Niger River. His achievement is in no way diminished by the fact that no record of his journey remains. Hornemann was the first European to cross the desert since the Romans.

Below: the castle of Marzūq, drawn by George Lyon in 1821, 23 years after Hornemann was there. Hornemann spent seven months in the area of Marzūq, but while he was there both he and Frendenburgh, his traveling companion, became sick. Frendenburgh died, but Hornemann managed to push on as far as the village of Bokani, near the Niger. There, in 1801, he too died.

Sansanding 1 Nov.r 1805.

Dear Megaw

Thunder, Death & Lightning:— the Devil to pay: lost by disease M.r Scott, two Sailors, four Carpenters & thirty one of the Royal African Corps, which reduces our numbers to seven, out of which Doctor Anderson & two of the Soldiers are quite useless. the former from one disease or other has been for four months disabled;— we every day suppose he'll kick it — Cap.t Park has not been unwell since we left Goree: I was one of the first taken sick of the fever & ague — had a hard pull for a few days; but my constitution soon got the better — had not an hours illness since — I send you for the information of the inquisitive, the names of the four men with me, viz Abraham Bolton, John Connor, Tho.s Higgins & Joseph Mills (the two last sick but recovering first — Higgins from a fever & Mills from an old wound in the ancle)

— Cap.t Park has made every enquiry concerning the River Niger, & from what he can learn there remains no doubt but it is the Congo — we hope to get there in about three Months or less — We had no fun on the road; — met no opposition the whole way — We were well received by Mansong, King of Sego; to whom Cap.t Park made very handsome presents, & at our arrival at the River, he sent Canoes upwards of 200 Miles to carry us & baggage, & also made us a present of one which we are now fitting out, as we intend going down the river in it — Cap.t P. is this day fixing the Masts &c — Schooner rigged — 40 feet long — 6 feet wide, & 5 feet high on the side all in the clear.— Excellent

P. e since we came here (Aug. 22) the Beef & Mutton

The Mystery of the Niger

9

Left: a letter from Lieutenant Martyn to a girl back home, describing the march under Mungo Park. At the time of this letter, the expedition had been underway almost six months and had reached Sansanding, where Park's brother-in-law, Anderson, had died. Below: a British soldier in the kind of uniform Park's men wore. It was totally unsuited to the climate and conditions which they encountered.

When Frederick Hornemann disappeared in 1800, the states of Europe were largely absorbed with the Napoleonic Wars. And until the Battle of Waterloo brought peace to Europe in 1815, there were no important developments in the exploration of the Niger. The one expedition that the British government did finance during those years resulted from a scare that Napoleon was about to expand his empire in Africa. In 1805, Mungo Park was invited to lead an expedition to sail along the Niger and somehow find the mouth of the river. In this way, the British government hoped to gain an important foothold in western Africa.

Park's second expedition was on a much grander scale than his first. On January 30, 1805, he and his brother-in-law Alexander Anderson sailed from Portsmouth well supplied with equipment and money. At Gorée, north of the Gambia River, they picked up a Lieutenant Martyn, 30 volunteer soldiers, 4 carpenters, and 2 sailors. Park himself had been given the rank and pay of a captain in the army, and Anderson, who was second-in-command, was made a lieutenant. The expedition also included a surgeon and a draughtsman.

With this large party, Park set out from the Gambia River in May, 1805. The soldiers, clad in the red coats then worn by the British Army on active duty, added a touch of color to the group. But unfortunately the rainy season was just beginning. Before very long the men began to suffer from the inevitable diseases—dysentery and malaria. But Park was ruthless, and determined to go on. Those of the party too ill to keep up with the rest were left behind to die. Only 10 men survived the dreadful journey to the Niger which they reached at Bamako in August, 1805.

Extracts from Park's diary convey something of the atmosphere of the trip. He seemed to have an indestructible will to carry on. "August 10, William Ashton declared that he was unable to travel. At half past four I arrived . . . at a stream flowing to the westwards. Here I found many of the soldiers sitting, and Mr. Anderson lying under a bush, apparently dying. Took him on my back, and carried him across the stream, which came up to my middle. Carried over the load of the ass which I drove, got over the ass, Mr. Anderson's horse, etc. Found myself much fatigued, having crossed the stream sixteen times. Left here four soldiers with their asses, being unable to carry over their loads . . . August 11th . . . This morning

Left: an Ibo canoe. It was from two such local craft that Mungo Park made his H.M.S. *Joliba.* In the *Joliba,* he and his party sailed down the Niger to the falls of Bussa. There they were ambushed, and all but one died.

Right: one of Mungo Park's last letters, written from Sansanding to Sir Joseph Banks. In this letter he explains the plan for the expedition's next stage: "It is my intention to keep [to] the middle of the River and make the best use I can of Winds and Currents till I reach the termination of this mysterious Stream."

Below: the early explorers found that the peoples of Africa had developed many highly skilled crafts. The sophisticated techniques of their metalworkers can be seen in these weapons made around Timbuktu.

hired Isaaco's people to go back and bring up the loads of soldiers who had halted by the side of the stream. In the course of the day all the loads arrived; but was sorry to find out that in the course of the last two marches we lost four men ... Cox, Cahill, Bird, and Ashton. Mr. Anderson still in a very dangerous way. ..."

Accompanied by his 10 survivors, Park got permission to pass through the Bambara territory. At Sansanding, they managed to build a large boat by breaking up two big local canoes. The H.M.S. *Joliba* (the local name for the Niger) was 40 feet long and 6 feet wide. Park filled it with all the provisions he could, so as to be able to sail down the river without having to stop for food. The party for the journey to the unknown mouth of the Niger consisted of Lieutenant Martyn, three soldiers, three slaves to paddle the boat, and a well-qualified, newly engaged guide and interpreter named Amadi Fatouma. Lieutenant Anderson had died during the two-month stay at Sansanding and Park's last letter to his wife, dated November 19, 1805, conveys the news of her brother's death.

On the day Park wrote to his wife he left Sansanding. For more than five years nothing more was heard about him. In 1810, the guide Isaaco, who had returned to Gambia with Park's letter to

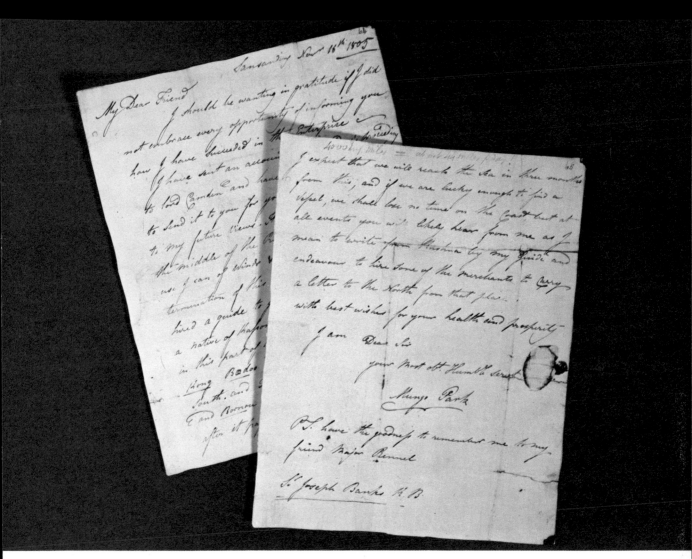

his wife, was sent out to discover what had happened to the missing *Joliba* and its party. He found Amadi Fatouma. On the journey down the Niger Fatouma had been captured by one of the kings through whose territory the *Joliba* had passed. He told Isaaco that not one of the Europeans had survived Park's expedition. He said that they had passed Kabara, the port of Timbuktu, and had managed to reach the falls of Bussa. The rapids were impassable because it was the season of low water before the monsoon (March or April, 1806), and the boat jammed in the rocks. The party was then attacked by Africans. Although they had until then been able to defend themselves with their muskets, this time the odds were too great. Park and Martyn tried to make a dash for it and jumped overboard into the rocks and shallow water, each carrying or helping one of the soldiers. They were, however, drowned during their desperate effort to escape. One of their slaves was taken prisoner, and it was he who told the story to Fatouma.

Mungo Park had shown, as well as exceptional physical strength and endurance, an outstanding courage and determination. With a little more luck the *Joliba* might have sailed on to the sea and found the mouth of the Niger River. But throughout the expedition

Above: the falls of Bussa, the place where a fierce army of Africans swept down on the *Joliba* which had become jammed in the rocky shallows The entire expedition, except for one slave, was killed in the attack.

Park made a number of serious mistakes. He should not have started the march from Gambia to Bamako in the rainy season. Later, when the *Joliba* was afloat, he should have taken a less hostile attitude toward the local tribesmen. Instead he did all he could to avoid them. When approached by African boats he fired at the crews and killed many men.

Mungo Park's imprisonment by the Moors at Benown during his first African expedition had made him very much aware of the kind of reception he was likely to meet on the journey down the Niger. He might have managed to get to the sea if he had been willing to be delayed and indulge in the customs of parleying and present-giving at the boundary of each small kingdom. (Ironically, before he got to the area of the falls at Bussa, Park had apparently presented a gift to a chieftain. But that chieftain had not passed on the present to the ruler of Bussa, who ordered the attack on Park's party.) As Park progressed down the Niger, he left destruction and bitterness. The hostility of the local tribesmen, who were not fanatically religious but were strongly opposed to the intrusion of Europeans was to remain a problem for succeeding explorers.

Because of the dangerous condition of the west coast approach to the Niger, the British government decided that future explorers should use the route from the north across the Sahara. In 1818, another Scottish doctor, Joseph Ritchie, was chosen to lead an expedition which included a naval captain, George Lyon, and a shipwright named Belford. They planned to travel through Tripoli to Fezzan so that they could estimate the prospects of travel farther south. They also intended to find out more about the course of the Niger River.

Almost immediately after they entered the desert, the three men caught malaria. At Marzūq, Ritchie died and Belford became dangerously ill. Although he recovered sufficiently to continue his journey with Lyon, the two men eventually decided that it was

Above: George Lyon in African dress. When he returned from Africa, Lyon stated firmly that for any serious attempt at exploration there an explorer would have to be able to travel disguised as a Moslem.

Below: a sand wind of the desert, drawn by George Lyon. Lyon accompanied Ritchie and Belford in an unsuccessful attempt to reach the Niger from Tripoli in 1818. Lyon did manage to travel more than 500 miles, but then ran out of money. He had to return across the desert with a slave caravan, and wrote an account of the appalling march.

hopeless to proceed. They joined a slave caravan to take them to the north again. On the way back, Lyon was appalled by what he saw of the transsaharan slave .trade and its brutalities. He found that many of the slaves believed they were being taken as cattle, to be slaughtered as meat for cannibals across the sea. Mungo Park had reported that slaves on the west coast destined for the West Indies and America had the same ghastly fear.

To his questions about the Niger, Lyon received confusing answers. He came to the conclusion that the river must enter Lake Chad and then flow on to join the Nile. He reported this mistaken theory to the British government—it was to influence the route of the next expedition. This time the plan was to go to Bornu, the kingdom around Lake Chad, by the caravan route that Hornemann had taken. This was the least difficult and dangerous of the ways across the Sahara because political links existed between Fezzan and Bornu. The Sultan of Bornu was at war with several neighboring states and managed to buy the support of the Sultan of Fezzan by allowing Fezzanese slave raids against his enemies.

A three-man team for the expedition to Bornu and Lake Chad was selected in London. The explorers were an Edinburgh doctor and

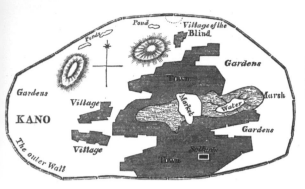

botanist, Walter Oudney; a naval lieutenant, also from Edinburgh, Hugh Clapperton; and an army officer, Dixon Denham. They left Tripoli early in 1822, and began their journey across the desert with a caravan of camels and equipment. But before they left Marzūq they too caught malaria. Although they were really too ill to cross the desert, Oudney, Clapperton, and Denham struggled on until they reached Lake Chad. The journey from Tripoli took them 11 months, but the result made it worthwhile. They were the first Europeans to see the lake.

At Kukawa, the capital of the Kingdom of Bornu, the party camped. They then explored the lake and concluded that it was not the key to the mystery of the Niger. None of the rivers flowing into the lake from the west was big enough to be the Niger, and no great river flowed out of it to the east.

Having found and explored Lake Chad, the party split up. Denham set off to the southeast to follow the Chari River. Clapperton and Oudney decided to make for the Niger by going west through the Hausa states. They joined a caravan traveling westward to Kano under the direction of a merchant named Fezzan. Clapperton and Oudney were still following in the footsteps of Hornemann, though his objective had been Katsina, not Kano. Oudney, however, died before they reached their destination. Clapperton pressed on to Kano, the capital of the Hausa kingdom and a trading center with a reputation as legendary as that of Timbuktu. During the journey Clapperton must have learned much about Kano from the merchants in the caravan and particularly from its leader. At first, Clapperton was disappointed with the city. But he soon became interested in the life around him. And he recorded numerous details about the life and customs of Kano.

On leaving Kano, Clapperton went on to Sokoto, the Fulani capital. Sokoto was a more powerful city than the older and more famous Kano. The ruler of the Fulani, Mohammed Bello, was the most powerful man in the whole of the western Sudan, and knew something of the outside world. He received Clapperton kindly, but refused to let him pursue his journey to the Niger, which was less than 150 miles away. When Clapperton asked about the course of the river, Mohammed Bello sketched in the sand a diagram showing the river entering the sea. But a map later shown to Clapperton, apparently drawn according to Bello's instructions, and perhaps

Above: Dixon Denham, an army major who had fought in the Battle of Waterloo. He took great pride in the fact that the expedition traveled "in our real character as Britons and Christians and [in] our English dress."

designed to confuse him, showed that the Niger flowed northeast to reach Egypt. Clapperton thought that this second map was a deliberate fake prepared to put him off going south to the river.

Mohammed Bello and his advisers put heavy pressure on Clapperton to dissuade him from pressing on to the Niger. It was perfectly true that the country was disturbed and that there would have been danger. However, all the evidence suggests that Mohammed Bello decided to discourage inquisitive strangers. But he was anxious to establish good relations with Britain, especially if they would enable him to improve trade, purchase muskets, and obtain a British physician for his court. Eventually, having convinced Clapperton of the futility of heading in any other direction, Mohammed Bello provided him with an escort and set him on the eastward road. He sent a letter to the British king with Clapperton, expressing his willingness to cooperate in ending the slave trade and a wish to establish trade with Britain.

On his return journey Clapperton met Denham at Kukawa. Denham had been searching for him. The trek from Lake Chad back to Tripoli through Marzūq took them from mid-September, 1824, to the end of January, 1825. Unluckily, in spite of all they had been through together, they disliked each other intensely. But there they were, alone together in the middle of the Sahara, forced to spend day after day in each other's company. It was a difficult situation for both men, and to make matters worse Clapperton was going back

Above: Bornu horsemen, riding across the desert today much as they would have done when Clapperton was at Mohammed Bello's court. The war Mohammed Bello was then waging with Bornu prevented Clapperton from continuing to the Niger.

Above: the reception of the mission by the Sultan of Bornu, as drawn by Dixon Denham. He reported that the sultan sat "in a sort of cage of cane or wood, near the door of his garden." Below: Hugh Clapperton, a naval lieutenant from Edinburgh, was the most important explorer in the party. His endurance must have been remarkable—he set out again for Africa after only two months in England.

to Tripoli without having reached the city of Timbuktu or even having gazed upon the Niger. Denham, too, became depressed by the intense hardships of the return journey. He wrote: "the fatigue and difficulty of a journey to Bornu are not to be compared with a return to Fezzan: the nine days from Izhya to Teghery, without either forage or wood, is distressing beyond description, to both camels and men, at the end of a journey such as this. . . ." At long last the two dejected explorers reached Tripoli.

In Tripoli, Clapperton learned from the British consul, Hanmer Warrington, that Alexander Laing had received official backing in London for a journey to the Niger. The government wanted Laing to travel across the Sahara. After reaching the great city, he was to go on and explore the Niger to its mouth. Clapperton was absolutely sure he had learned the secret of the Niger from the map which Mohammed Bello had originally drawn in the sand. He felt convinced that if only he could get to the Niger, he could sail to the sea. It would be a bitter disappointment to be forestalled by Laing.

Back in London, Clapperton's success in reaching Kano made him famous. The letter he carried from the sultan also impressed the government officials. Two months after his arrival in England from Tripoli, Hugh Clapperton sailed for Africa in H.M.S. *Brazen* with a party consisting of two doctors, two black servants, a Captain Pearce, and Richard Lander, who was Clapperton's manservant. By November, 1825, they had reached the Bight of Benin and had landed at Badagri on the coast of what is now Nigeria. By the time Clapperton had journeyed 200 miles inland, three of his English companions, including Pearce, had died of malaria, and he was alone with Lander.

By coincidence, Clapperton's route northward to Sokoto took him past the falls of Bussa where Mungo Park had died. There he first saw the Niger. He crossed the river and struggled on northeastward to Kano. From Kano, he traveled on to Sokoto, where Mohammed Bello was involved in a new war against Bornu, but was no longer interested in entering diplomatic relations with England. Bello was still against Clapperton's continuing to the Bornu country. And he was also opposed to Clapperton's having anything to do with the enemies of the Fulani. It eventually transpired that Bello was really upset about the letters of introduction and presents for the Sultan of Bornu which Clapperton and Lander had in their baggage. At an audience with the Sultan in February, 1827, the Sultan agrees to send Clapperton to the sea by way of the Niger. Success was in sight. But soon afterward, Clapperton became very ill with malaria and dysentery. In March, he was completely incapacitated by dysentery and had to be looked after constantly by Lander. In spite of Lander's care he died on April 13, 1827.

The death of Clapperton left Lander in a very difficult situation. He was now completely without anyone he could trust. He was also deep in country where the local tribesmen were hostile to European travelers. His duty to Clapperton was to return to England with his

Left: the town of Kano, drawn by Heinrich Barth, the German explorer who was in the town 25 years after Clapperton's second visit there. From Kano, Clapperton went on to Mohammed Bello's court. He found Bello once again at war with Bornu.

papers. Lander did not trust the Arabs with whom he would have to travel if he went north across the desert. He badly wanted to try to find the Niger and trace its course, but it was now May and the rainy season. He did set out toward the upper Niger, but gave up any idea of exploring the river and returned to Kano. From Kano, accompanied by only one slave and a servant boy, he made his way back to Badagri. There, he boarded a ship for home. Lander was back in England at the end of April, 1828, a year after Clapperton's death. He delivered his master's papers to the officials in London and then began to write an account of their adventures.

Lander was a determined young man and was greatly fired with

Above: a member of the Dawada tribe, which Clapperton visited. They lived then as now around salt lakes, fishing for what they describe as worms—in fact a kind of shrimp. They live on these shrimps and dates.

the idea of African exploration. He managed to convince the government of his sincerity and ability to trace the course of the Niger from Bussa to the sea. He received official backing for such an expedition, and at the end of January, 1830, he left England again, this time with his brother John. They had arrived at Bussa by the end of May, but did not begin their journey by canoe down river until the end of September. By mid-November the Landers had reached the coast at a small settlement called Brass Town.

The task which Mungo Park had set out to accomplish in 1805

Above: Richard Lander. He was from Cornwall, and went to Africa as Clapperton's manservant. After Clapperton's death, he managed to get himself out of the interior and reached England again in April, 1828. Below: John Lander. He joined his brother on the expedition which was finally successful in tracing the course of the Niger River from Bussa, where Park had died, to the sea.

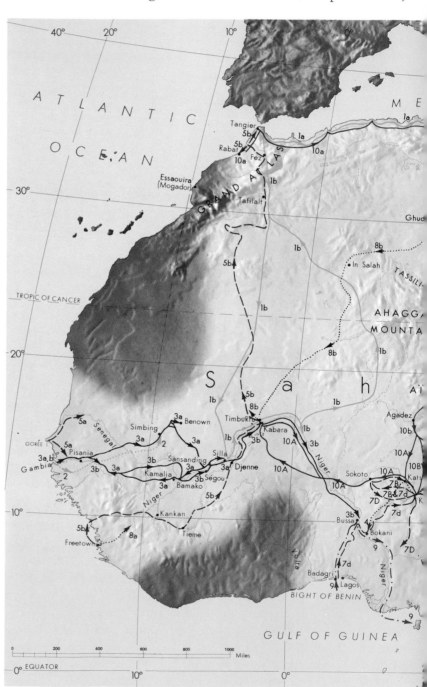

was now complete. The mouth of the Niger had been discovered, and the river's course was known from Bamako to the coast. Though the British no longer needed to forestall Napoleon's plans, they had all the same gained a foothold in western Africa which they had sought so long ago. Now they could expand their trade in the area, and could at last attempt to end the brutal traffic in slaves. More than 50 years were to pass before the true start of the colonial era. When that age dawned the long-standing British presence on the Niger helped to bring the entire area under European rule.

Below: northern Africa, showing the routes of explorers in the Sahara and the Niger region. Toward the end of the 1700's, European adventurers became interested in exploring the Niger region, and in tracing the river's course. Some chose to reach the Niger from the west coast of Africa. Others crossed the Sahara to the river. In so doing they carried out the first exploration of the vast desert.

Ibn-Batuta (part of journey)	1a	1325–32
Ibn-Batuta	1b	1349–53
Houghton	2	1790–1
Park	3a	1795–7
	3b	1805–6
Hornemann	4	1798–1801
Caillie	5a	1816–1824
	5b	1827–8
Ritchie & Lyon	6	1818
Clapperton (with Oudney & Denham)	7a	1822–5
Clapperton (with Oudney)	7A	1822
Clapperton (after death of Oudney)	7B	1823–4
Denham	7C	1823–4
Clapperton (with R. Lander)	7d	1825–7
Lander R. (after death of Clapperton)	7D	1827–8
Laing	8a	1822
	8b	1825–6
Lander, R. (with J. Lander)	9	1830–2
Barth	10a	1845–7
Barth (with Richardson & Overweg)	10b	1850–5
Barth (after explorers separated)	10A	
Overweg	10B	
Richardson	10C	

© Geographical Projects

123

Timbuktu, the Lure of Legend

10

Left: Alexander Laing on patrol in Sierra Leone. He was born and educated in Scotland. He first planned to become a schoolteacher, but his love of adventure led him to join the army. While serving in West Africa, Laing became interested in exploring the Niger, and discovering its true mouth.

Above: the typical clothing of women in Tripoli at the time that Laing was in the city preparing for his expedition across the desert. It was during his stay that he fell in love with the British consul's daughter.

Clapperton's rival in the race to explore the Niger to its mouth was a Scotsman, Major Alexander Laing. Laing's interest in exploring the interior of Africa began when he was stationed in Sierra Leone in western Africa. During his tour of duty there, he became convinced that there could not possibly be a junction of the Niger and the Nile rivers. He was sure that the least popular theory was correct—that the Niger eventually flowed into the Atlantic. By the spring of 1825, the young Scotsman, with the backing of the British government, was on his way to the north coast of Africa in an attempt to prove his theory right.

In Tripoli, Laing was delayed by sickness. He was anxious to move on, but the British consul, Hanmer Warrington—the man who had informed Clapperton about Laing's projected journey— urged Laing to rest and get well before going on to Timbuktu.

During this period of enforced rest, Laing spent much of his time with Warrington's daughter Emma and eventually fell in love with her. Warrington considered that "a more wild, enthusiastic and romantic attachment never before existed," but he did not succeed in discouraging his daughter from marrying Laing. After their marriage, Laing started his risky journey.

Laing set off on July 18, 1825. His journey became a race with Clapperton to reach Timbuktu—he was fully aware of Clapperton's plans, and the rivalry was mutual. He left Tripoli accompanied by a small caravan, his servant Jack Le Bore, two West Indian boatbuilders, and an interpreter. He was well provided with funds, and carried with him an impressive letter of introduction to the Sultan of Timbuktu.

Two months after leaving Tripoli, the caravan reached the oasis of Ghudāmis. It was less than 300 miles from Tripoli, but Laing had had to make a detour of 600 miles to avoid a local war. He was continually plagued by inquisitive and greedy tribesmen who forced him to pay bribes. The Turkish clothes which he had brought with him and eventually began wearing did little to make the journey easier. In spite of his treatment, Laing liked Ghudāmis very much. But as each day passed he became more depressed by a sense of loneliness and isolation. He worried about his guides and money and felt generally bitter about the lack of concern with which he seemed to be regarded by officials in London. There was also his intense longing for his wife, Emma.

Above: Alexander Laing. Laing was not a strong man, and throughout his life was plagued by ill health. His expedition to Timbuktu proved that he had the will to endure crushing hardship. Nevertheless the great loneliness of desert travel preyed on his mind and, he was constantly worried about the hostility of the nomad tribes.

The journey from Ghudāmis to the next oasis, In Salah, took Laing and his party a month and led them into the very heart of the Sahara. The caravan was outside any protection the Pasha of Tripoli could give, and was completely dependent on the nomad Tuareg tribes who controlled the desert routes. Laing wrote: "Whatever they demand, must be given them; a refusal would be a signal for plunder and murder; but if once satisfied they will . . . be your guides and protectors through their desert, dreary country. . . ." At In Salah, Laing was received with amazement by the natives, who had never set eyes on a European before. At one point he was requested to appear on the roof of his house so that he could be

seen by as many as possible of the fascinated townspeople.

A rumor began to spread through the town that Laing was in fact Mungo Park. A Moslem who had been wounded in one of the clashes with the *Joliba* was prepared to swear that Laing was the man who had been in command. The rumor naturally made Laing realize how unwise Park had been to leave such a trail of hostility behind him in his journey down the Niger. He was afraid that the Africans would become more hostile as he drew nearer the river, and that his journey would be even more dangerous than he had feared.

Nearly everything that is known of Laing's trek comes from the

Above: the typical Sahara terrain which Laing described in one letter as "provokingly monotonous." The distinctive desert plants, which look like dead brown sticks when dry, turn green when even a little rain falls. They provided almost the only source of food for the camels then used by all the travelers in the desert.

letters he sent back to Tripoli by courier. He was obviously worried about his safety even at In Salah. There, the Tuareg were irritated by the presence of a Christian who could speak only a few words of Arabic. Though his letters reveal little of the hardships of day-to-day life, we do know from them that his departure from In Salah was delayed because of rumors of the capture of another caravan to Timbuktu.

At last, in early January, 1826, a large caravan, including Laing's party, left In Salah. The route through the desert had no sizable oases or resting places. In his enthusiasm Laing had no idea of Timbuktu's exact position or that it was still nearly 900 miles farther on across the desert.

After two or three weeks of difficult travel, Laing's section of the caravan was attacked by a band of Tuareg tribesmen. Laing was severely wounded and only three members of his party survived. The caravan would not wait to accompany the wounded men to Timbuktu, but nevertheless they managed to travel some 400 miles across the desert to the lands of a friendly Arab chieftain called Sidi Mohammed Muktar. Sidi Mohammed treated Laing with great generosity and kindness, and the wounded man spent four months with him. While he was there, however, a plague he described as similar to yellow fever struck the town, killing all three remaining

Below: desert Arabs exercising, drawn by George Lyon some time before Laing's expedition. Laing soon encountered the aggressiveness and then warlike spirit of the Tuareg nomads.

members of the party, and the Arab chieftain Sidi Mohammed. Laing, too, nearly died of the disease. When he had recovered, he arranged for a guide to take him on to Timbuktu.

Early in August, 1826, Alexander Laing arrived at the far side of the desert, and on August 13 he entered Timbuktu. He had traveled 2,650 miles since leaving Tripoli and had endured countless difficulties and hardships.

There is one letter from Timbuktu in existence, written to "Consul Warrington and My dear Emma." It contains news of Laing's arrival in Timbuktu and his plans for leaving. He wrote:

Above: a Timbuktu water hole. Laing expected Timbuktu to be a great metropolis, but all he found was a small slave market in an un-distinguished town. He had great difficulty in leaving Timbuktu as hostile Arabs surrounded the town.

Above: a caravan moves across the desert at night. It was with such a caravan that Laing left Timbuktu. On the third night, the sheik under whose protection Laing was traveling killed him and his servant as they slept. The bodies were left under a tree, and the caravan moved on.

". . . my situation in Timbuktu [has been] rendered exceedingly unsafe by the unfriendly disposition of the Foolahs of Massine, who have this year upset the dominion of the Tuaric & made themselves patrons of Timbuctu & as a party of Foolahs are hourly expected, Al Kaidi Boubokar, who is an excellent good man, & who trembles for my safety, has strongly urged my immediate departure, and I am sorry to say that the notice has been so short, and I have so much to do previous to going away, that this is the only communication I shall for the present be able to make. My destination is Sego [Ségou], whither I hope to arrive in fifteen days, but I regret to say that the road is a vile one and my perils are not yet at an end, but my trust is in God Who has hitherto bore me up amidst the severest trials & protected me amid the numerous dangers to which I have been exposed. . . ."

Despite Al Kaidi's warning, and his own plans for a speedy

departure, Laing stayed five weeks in Timbuktu. He had freedom to go about as he wished, making notes for his journal. But there was always the problem of how to get out of the city safely. It was almost completely surrounded by unfriendly tribesmen. He was urged by leaders in the city to return to Tripoli by the way he had come. Laing, however, persisted in his wish to go out by a southwest route which would take him through hostile country.

Late in September, 1826, Laing joined a small caravan going toward Arouan. According to tribesmen in that area, the third night out from Timbuktu he and his Arab servant boy were killed by the fanatical sheik who had charge of the caravan in which they were traveling. The bodies were left beneath a tree and all of Laing's baggage was burned.

In March, 1827, six months after Alexander Laing's murder and just a few weeks before Clapperton's death at Sokoto, a Frenchman named René Caillié set out from Sierra Leone for Timbuktu. He was hoping to be the first Frenchman to reach the famous city and so receive a prize of 10,000 francs which was being offered by the French Geographical Society.

Born the son of a poor baker, Caillié had been fascinated by stories of travel almost as soon as he had learned to read. As he grew up he began to study geography books and maps. It was the map of Africa which particularly excited him. On it he saw nothing

Below: the French official enquiry of 1910 digging for Laing's remains. After the murders, a passing Arab had buried the bodies. The nephew of the sheik who had killed Laing was still alive, but by then 82 years old. He still possessed the golden brooch which the sheik had taken from the explorer's body—it had been a parting gift from Laing's wife, Emma.

Above: René Caillié. The son of a baker who had died in prison, Caillié had a passion for travel from the time he was small. He had no particular scientific interest in exploration, but he was determined to be the first Frenchman to reach Timbuktu.

but desert or areas marked "unknown". Very soon his interest in reading about Africa developed into a passion to explore it.

At the age of 16, Caillié got a job as a servant on a French ship which was going to Senegal. From Senegal, he eventually managed to join an expedition which had been organized to go inland to search for any sign of Mungo Park's second expedition on the Niger. During this time, Caillié had also got hold of a copy of Park's account of his first journey. This strengthened his desire to explore the interior of Africa himself, and he began working to save money for the journey. He went to live for nine months in a primitive Moorish village called Brakna, where he learned to speak Arabic and studied the Koran. The stories he had heard and read about the hostility of Moslems toward European travelers had made him realize that he would have to travel as a Moslem. When he left Brakna, Caillié could pass as an Arab.

After he had saved some money, Caillié was able to buy the supplies he would need for the journey to Timbuktu. In March, 1827, he embarked at Freetown in Sierra Leone. His destination was the Rio Nunez estuary between Sierra Leone and Senegal. From there he would proceed inland. He traveled as an Arab and explained to his guides and companions that he had been born in Egypt, where he had been captured and deported by the French. Now he was on his way to make the pilgrimage to Mecca and search for his family.

Caillié arrived at the Rio Nunez nine days after leaving Freetown. After a few miles he managed to join a caravan which was going to Timbuktu. Early in June the caravan reached the Niger at Kouroussa. There Caillié and his three servants joined another caravan which would take them to Kankan and Djenné. Fever had already begun to attack him, but he managed to keep up with the caravan which was very much delayed by continual crossings of the tributaries of the Niger. In his journal Caillié seldom mentions his difficulties during this period, but concentrates instead on noting the names of places.

In August, Caillié walked wearily into the town of Tieme which— unknown to him—was less than a quarter of the way to Timbuktu. There he developed scurvy and was unfortunate enough to catch malaria as well. To add to his troubles, his foot was very painful and he was unable to walk. He was taken into a primitive grass

Right: a drawing of the Niger River taken from René Caillié's own book. This was probably Caillié's very first sight of the Niger River on his journey across Africa on the way to Timbuktu. Caillié started his journey from the west coast of Africa.

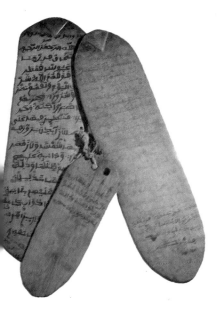

Above: Koran boards from the Mandingo area, near Timbuktu. Caillié spent nine months in a Moorish village, preparing for his journey by studying the Koran and learning Arab and African customs. When he left there, he could pass as an Arab. Below: Caillié in Arab dress. Not everyone he met believed that he was really an Arab, but all the same he was generally received kindly.

hut at Tieme and cared for by an old Negro woman, who kept him alive for five months.

"I soon experienced all the horrors of that dreadful disease [scurvy]. The roof of my mouth became quite bare, a part of the bones exfoliated [peeled off] and fell away, and my teeth seemed ready to drop out of their sockets. I feared that my brain would be affected by the agonizing pains I felt in my head, and I was more than a fortnight without sleep. To crown my misery, the sore in my foot broke out afresh and all hope of my departure vanished. . . . Alone, in the interior of a wild country, stretched on the damp ground, with no pillow but the leather bag which contained my luggage, with no medicine. . . . This good creature [the old Negro woman] brought me twice a day a little rice water, which she forced me to drink, for I could eat nothing. I soon reduced to a skeleton. . . . Suffering had deprived me of all energy. One thought alone absorbed my mind—that of Death. I wished for it, and prayed for it to God."

Despite Caillié's prayers, the old Negro's care eventually had its effect. In January, 1828, with a new guide, he was fit enough to continue his journey. In early March he arrived at Djenné. He was just a little more than 200 miles from Timbuktu. Caillié had walked nearly all the way—1,000 miles. During his journey he had received kind treatment from Moslem and non-Moslem alike.

At Djenné, which is situated on a tributary of the Niger, Caillié boarded a boat for Timbuktu. This proved to be the worst experience of his journey. He was very sick much of the time. He was also ranked with slaves and forced to lie in the most cramped quarters below deck. When they entered the country where the Tuareg roamed the banks of the river, Caillié had to remain out of

sight below deck during the day. After a month of dreadful heat and fear of being discovered by the Tuareg, he caught sight of Kabara, the port of Timbuktu. His first glimpse of the city of Timbuktu a few hours later proved to be an unexpected anticlimax.

"I looked around and found that the sight before me did not answer my expectations. I had formed a totally different idea of the grandeur and wealth of Timbuktu . . . the city presented, at first view, nothing but a mass of ill-looking houses, built of earth. Nothing was to be seen in all directions but immense plains of quicksand of a yellowish-white color. The sky was a pale red as far as the horizon; all nature wore a dreary aspect, and the most profound silence prevailed; not even the warbling of a bird was to be heard."

Caillié strolled round the city the next day. Timbuktu was a

Above: a drawing of Timbuktu from the book by René Caillié. Like Laing, he found that the famous city was a typical desert town, not particularly wealthy, and less impressive than other towns he had traveled through. He complained that "Timbuktu and its environs present the most monotonous and barren scene I ever beheld."

dying place. Little business was being done, and unlike Djenné, the streets were empty of foreign travelers. "I was surprised," says Caillié, "at the inactivity, I might even say, indolence, displayed in the city." He saw three shops, which were really small rooms, with good stocks of European cloth, and also a warehouse with European merchandise, including muskets. But there was no local agriculture whatsoever, and the city's only substantial source of income was as a distributing center for the salt brought in from the mines in the far north.

Caillié's lodgings were opposite the house where Laing had stayed, and he made such discreet enquiries about Laing's death as he could without arousing too much suspicion. He spent much time studying and sketching architectural details of the three principal mosques in the city.

Caillié's visit lasted for two weeks. He left on May 4 for Morocco with a caravan of 1,200 camels, numerous slaves, and other merchandise. Four days out from Timbuktu the scene of Laing's murder was pointed out to him by members of the party.

During his arduous journey across the Sahara, Caillié encountered all the horrors of desert travel. He experienced such thirst that he thought of nothing but water, and would go about begging for an extra mouthful to add to the tiny ration issued in the evening to each member of the caravan. Besides, his disguise was now becoming less convincing, probably because of the stress of the intolerable conditions. His guide was a malicious and mischievous individual who teased Caillié and gave him ridiculous nicknames. The guide and his companions further terrified the Frenchman by saying that he looked like a Christian. This taunting naturally made him think of Laing's death. Finally they reached the oasis of Tafilalt on the south side of the Grand Atlas on July 23, 1828. Caillié was another six weeks getting across the Atlas through Fez and Rabat to reach Tangier, where he could ask the help of the French consul.

It was not easy, however, to prove to the French authorities that he really had gone to Timbuktu. They eventually acknowledged his claim, but only after a special committee had been formed to investigate it. Back in France, Caillié received the award of 10,000 francs from the Geographical Society. He was the first Frenchman to have reached the city of legendary wealth and the first man to have survived to tell of his experiences there.

Above: the house in which René Caillié lived in Timbuktu—it is opposite the house where Laing stayed. Above the door a plaque has been placed commemorating the fact that Caillié lived there. The French held the city for many years, and placed several such plaques in memory of early explorers.

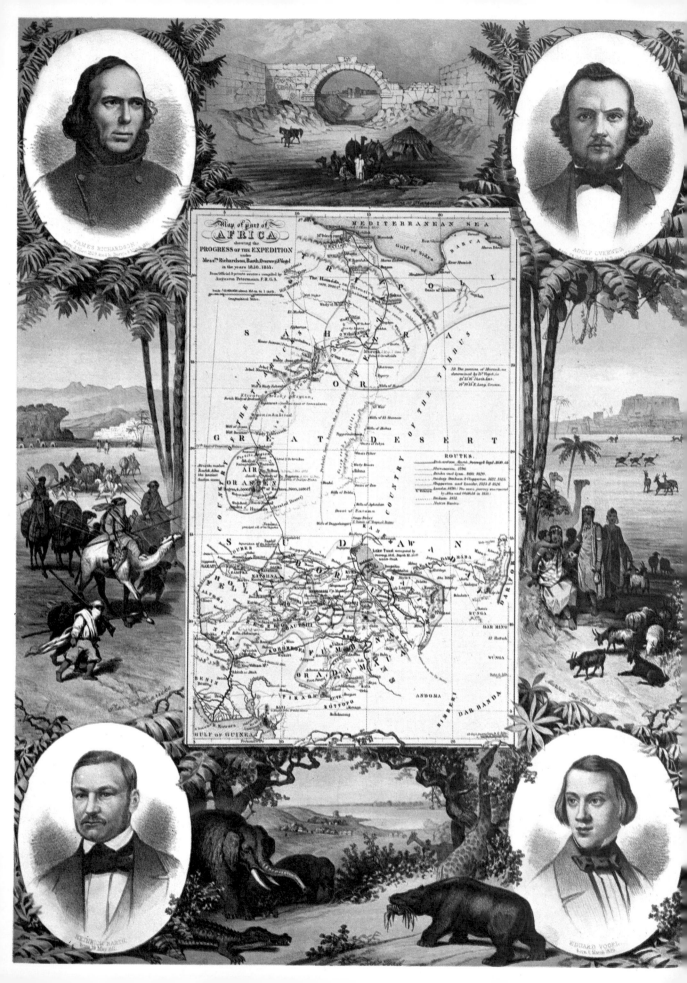

Conquering the Sahara

11

Left: an 1854 map of Africa, showing the portraits and routes of Richardson (top left); Barth (bottom left); Overweg (top right); and Vogel (bottom right). The other pictures show scenes reported by the four explorers.

During the 50 years that followed René Caillié's return from Timbuktu, a succession of travelers tried to cross the Sahara to Timbuktu and the other cities along the Niger. Many of those who attempted this journey never came back. Of about 200 who set out, 165 died from disease or were killed by the Tuareg. But those who did survive the terrible hardships of the desert brought back reports and information which would eventually help to open up barren wastes of the Sahara.

Many of the unsuccessful Saharan travelers in the 1800's were wealthy young men who engaged in semiscientific exploration in many parts of the world. Typical of these explorers was a British doctor, John Davidson. He had already traveled widely in eastern Europe and North and Central America before he turned his attention to the Sahara. His plan was to cross the desert by the caravan route through the wasteland of Mauritania. Davidson was warned that he had chosen a very dangerous route, and that, at that time, the hazards were made worse by tribal fighting. But he would not be put off. In 1836 he set out from Mogador (now Essaouira), on the coast of Morocco, and had traveled barely six weeks with a caravan when he was killed.

It seems probable that Davidson's murderers were paid by powerful Arab merchants, worried that their monopoly of that caravan route would be broken if Europeans were allowed to interfere. The Arab merchants had good reason for their fears. During the 1800's, merchants in Europe—and particularly in Britain—became increasingly interested in the caravan routes across the Sahara, and in the possibilities for trade in that part of Africa. But the next European to venture across the burning sands was employed, not by merchants, but by a British Bible society whose chief aim was to find out more about the slave trade across the Sahara. That man was James Richardson. He set out from Tripoli in August, 1845, traveling openly as a European and a Christian, and first headed southwest to the oasis of Ghudāmis. From there, he struck due south, nearly 400 miles to the city of Ghāt. There he was warmly welcomed by the sultan, who gave him presents to take back to Queen Victoria. After observing and recording details of the slave trade, Richardson set out on the return trek to the Mediterranean coast, where he took a ship to London. Although his journey had been a limited one—he had penetrated only about 700 miles into the

Above: James Richardson, wearing the costume of the people of Ghudāmis. He did not attempt to disguise himself for his journey, but traveled openly as a European as far as Ghāt, about 600 miles from Tripoli.

Below: the antislavery convention of 1840. Notice that there is a Negro in the audience. The horrors of the slave trade in Africa struck each of the explorers with enormous force. Their reports gave a new impulse to demands for the abolition of slavery, but even after slavery was officially abolished, slaving continued in Africa. Below right: a gang of Negro slaves with their Arab captors. This Victorian engraving shows a mother and child dying on the ground, while the vultures wheel overhead.

Sahara—Richardson's account of his travels aroused great interest in London. In particular, his reports of the cruelties of the slave trade stirred up strong feelings in Britain.

The British government now became interested in the idea of investigating the great caravan routes between the oases of the Sahara and the cities on the southern fringe of the desert. A few years after Richardson's return, they authorized an official expedition to explore these routes and to gain more information about the slave trade. They appointed Richardson to lead the expedition. Richardson wanted to make his team as international as possible. He also wanted to recruit men with a more scientific approach to African exploration than the romantic adventurers of the past.

The Prussian ambassador in London suggested to Richardson the name of a young German, Heinrich Barth, who already had experience of exploration in the Middle East and in northern Africa. Barth had studied archaeology, history, geography, and law at the University of Berlin. He had also spent some time in London learning Arabic. He seemed an ideal candidate, and Richardson quickly asked him to join the expedition. Barth eagerly agreed, and at once began

Left: a drawing of Ghāt by Heinrich Barth. He spent five years in all traveling around the southern fringe of the Sahara between Lake Chad and Timbuktu. Barth was a methodical, humorless, and unemotional man who was well prepared, physically and practically, for his African adventure. He allowed nothing to deter him.

Below: the *monster of Sefar,* one of the notable Neolithic rock paintings found in the Tassili-n-Ajjer.

a strenuous course of physical training to get himself in good shape for the rigorous months ahead. The third member of Richardson's party was a young German geologist named Adolf Overweg.

The expedition which left Tripoli in 1850 appears to have been the best organized and equipped ever to have ventured across the Sahara. The three Europeans were accompanied by the usual retinue of guides and servants. They had with them great quantities of stores and equipment, including a large wooden boat in which they planned to explore Lake Chad. The boat was in two sections to make it easier to carry.

The explorers themselves were particularly well suited to the job in hand. Barth especially was very well trained, and Richardson, the leader, was familiar with the desert and its dangers. Unfortunately, soon after they set out these two men seem to have developed a strong personal dislike for each other. From the beginning the party was split into distinct national groups. During the heat of the day the two Germans rode ahead, followed at a considerable distance by Richardson and a British sailor who had been sent along to manage the boat. Even in the cool of the evening the two groups and their servants settled down to eat and sleep in separate camps.

In this unfriendly atmosphere the party arrived in Marzūq in May, 1850. From there they went on to Ghāt. A few days out from Ghāt, Barth decided to climb the mysterious Mount Idinen, which according to the Tuareg was inhabited by evil spirits. He reached the summit of the mountain but was so exhausted and thirsty that, by the time he made his descent, he had drunk all of the water he had with him. He then lost his way and eventually fell to the ground in a state of semiconsciousness. On regaining his senses, he managed to prevent himself from panicking, and cut open one of his veins to quench his thirst by drinking his own blood. A Tuareg found him and helped him to get back to Overweg and the expedition. His companions bound up his wound and Barth quickly recovered.

From Ghāt the party traveled through the Tassili-n-Ajjer where, nearly a century later, thousands of Neolithic rock paintings were to be discovered. Barth himself saw some rock carvings there. The party had a rough passage through the mountains. They were frequently attacked by marauders, forced to pay ransom money, and even so had to defend themselves by firing on their attackers. As they made their way through the Aïr Mountains they were threatened

by the hostile Tuareg tribesmen, who demanded that they renounce their Christian religion or die by sundown. Luckily the Tuareg were willing to strike a bargain, and their religious fervor evaporated when they were offered one-third of the belongings of the British expedition.

From the Aïr Mountains Barth traveled south to Agadez, once one of the great centers of commerce in the Sahara. By the mid-1800's, however, Agadez' prosperity had declined and Barth describes it as an abandoned city whose population had dwindled from 50,000 to 7,000. Everywhere he saw traces of vanished splendor.

It was soon after this that the three men decided to separate. Richardson headed directly for Lake Chad, and the two Germans set off to find a more westerly route to the lake. Shortly afterward, Barth parted from Overweg, and made an expedition on his own to Katsina and Kano. The three men had arranged to meet at Kukawa in April, 1851. But Richardson never kept the rendezvous. Three weeks before Barth arrived at Kukawa to meet his companions, Richardson died of fever.

Overweg was the last of the party to reach Lake Chad. When he finally arrived there in May he was exhausted and suffering from fever. Nevertheless, while Barth explored the territory to the south and east of Lake Chad, Overweg recovered sufficiently to explore the lake itself in the boat they had brought with them across the Sahara. The two men stayed for about 15 months in the Lake Chad region. When the British government heard that Richardson had died, they appointed Barth the new leader of the expedition. They also sent sufficient funds for the two men to continue to their next objective—Timbuktu. But before they started on this stretch of their journey, Overweg died of malaria. He was only 29 years old.

Barth, too, had suffered numerous attacks of dysentery and fever. But, despite his own illnesses and the deaths of Richardson and Overweg, he was determined to go on. At the end of November, 1852, he left the capital of Bornu. He had now been 32 months on the journey out from Tripoli. He knew the next stretch to Timbuktu might take him another two years. Barth was confident, however, that he would reach his destination. He was certainly fortunate in his dealings with local tribesmen, and he attributes his luck to a single incident. One day when he was surrounded by a hostile group of fierce-looking townspeople, Barth fired off six rounds from his

Above: Barth's drawing of the interior of a Mugsu dwelling. Barth initially specified that he would undertake only scientific work on the expedition. However, after Richardson's death, he was appointed leader, and, although a German, he became Britain's representative. The expedition was to investigate routes across the Sahara, and to learn more about the slave trade.

revolver into the air. In his journal he says that this show of force had great influence over his future safety. The Africans were afraid, believing he had guns hidden in all his pockets and could fire them as and when he wished.

When Barth finally reached Timbuktu in September, 1853, he found the city slightly more prosperous than Caillié had done 25 years earlier. But it had never regained the position as a trading center for the Sahara that it had held in the 1500's and before.

Early in 1854 Barth left Timbuktu and began working his way eastward to Lake Chad. On the way he learned that a party of Europeans had been sent out by the British government to look for him and had already arrived at the lake. This party was led by another German, Edward Vogel, who when he met Barth explained that people in London had given him up for dead. After a brief discussion, it was decided that Barth should go on to Kukawa. Vogel, meanwhile, would make for Zinder, a town almost 300 miles west of Lake Chad. He was to rejoin Barth before starting the journey north across the desert.

Barth, however, eventually made the desert crossing without Vogel — the latter decided to stay in Africa and explore the Lower Niger. Barth left for the desert in May, 1855, and, despite the fact that it was the hottest time of the year, he managed to get back to

Tripoli and on to London by early September. He had been away over five years. Vogel was murdered in 1856 on his way to the Nile.

The success of the British expedition of 1850–1855 was due almost entirely to Barth's single-mindedness. Despite innumerable difficulties and the very real threat of death from the fanatically religious tribesmen, he fulfilled his mission, and brought back a vast amount of information about northern Africa. It was Barth's scientific thoroughness which made him unique—no other explorer of the same area managed to accomplish as much as he had. He was the first man to make reliable maps of huge areas of Africa, and the first man to study the customs of the Negro tribes he encountered.

Barth was to have great influence on all future explorers of the Sahara. And he was most generous in giving them the benefit of his advice and encouragement. Three Germans—Gerhard Rohlfs, Gustav Nachtigal, and Oscar Lenz—and a Frenchman—Henri Duveyrier—are probably the most important of his successors.

Gerhard Rohlfs was a German soldier who, in order to prepare himself for travel in the desert, joined the Foreign Legion in Algiers. In 1862, he disguised himself as a religious official and set out for the interior of Morocco. On this first journey Rohlfs traveled to the oasis of Tafilalt—he was the first European since René Caillié to report on this area. Rohlf's second journey was far more ambitious. From Tafilalt he pushed southeastward to In Salah, in the very heart of the desert. Rohlf's dream was to visit Timbuktu, but at In Salah he ran short of money and was forced to abandon his plan. Instead he traveled north through Ghudāmis to Tripoli.

Below: a drawing based on the reports of Edward Vogel, a young German who was sent by the British government to look for Heinrich Barth. His descriptions of the vegetation of the Chad area were highly imaginative.

The second German expedition to the Sahara resulted from King Wilhelm of Prussia's desire to join the European race for trade and influence in Africa. He commissioned Gustav Nachtigal to cross the Sahara with numerous elaborate presents for the Sultan of Bornu—Nachtigal needed eight camels simply to carry the gifts. However, he made the journey across the Sahara safely, and reported that the Sultan was delighted with the presents. Nachtigal was an explorer as well as an envoy. He traveled widely in the Tibesti Massif, and also managed to visit Darfur and Kordofan (in the west

Above: Gustav Nachtigal, who traveled across the Sahara carrying with him the most remarkable collection of presents from the King of Prussia to the Sultan of Bornu. Nachtigal was fortunate to arrive unmolested.

of what is now Sudan), and explore the valley of the Nile.

Oscar Lenz's achievement was to cross the Sahara from Morocco to the mouth of the Senegal River—in effect, this was very like Caillié's route, but in reverse. With only a small party, Lenz made good time, and only 40 days or so after leaving the slopes of the Grand Atlas he arrived at Timbuktu. To his great astonishment he was well received there, and the 18 days he spent in the city were, he says, among the best in his life. From his account, it is clear that Timbuktu was still in decline, although the political situation was less tense. Lenz left Timbuktu in mid-July, 1880, and by November he had reached a French outpost on the Senegal River.

Perhaps the most famous of all Barth's successors was Henri Duveyrier. Duveyrier first visited North Africa in 1857 when he was 17 years old. He was fascinated by what he saw, and returned to France determined to prepare himself properly for a more ambitious expedition. He traveled first to London, to get Barth's advice, and to continue his studies of geology, natural sciences, and languages.

In 1859, when he was still only 19 years old, Duveyrier set out from the French colony of Algeria for the oasis of El Goléa, which was a stronghold of Moslem tribesmen. When he finally reached there, the Moslems drove him away from the oasis and threatened to kill him if he came back. But in spite of this treatment, Duveyrier refused to show any sign of fear in his dealings with the tribesmen.

His courage even succeeded in the end in winning their respect.

Duveyrier next went south from Tripoli to the Tassili-n-Ajjer, where he made friends with two powerful Ajjer chiefs. He lived a year among the Ajjer Tuareg, sharing their hard way of life, and learning their language and writing. During this time he remained fascinated by the people—he took copious notes and asked questions on every subject relating to their way of life.

When Duveyrier eventually returned to Tripoli, he had in mind another expedition to the Tuareg of the Ahaggar Mountains. But before he carried out his plan, he returned to Paris. There he edited his notes and fitted himself out with new equipment. He had hardly finished writing up his notes when he became ill with a recurrence of typhoid fever, which he had first contracted while living with the Tuareg. He temporarily lost his memory and from that time onward was unable to continue any serious explorations. Neverthe-

Above: a water hole, drawn by Barth. The lives of explorers in the desert depended on oases and water holes, and if, as often happened, a water hole went dry, the party faced almost certain death from thirst.

Left: Henri Duveyrier (1840–1892) went to Africa and lived among the Tuareg, sharing their difficult life. He refused to be afraid of them, and succeeded in gaining their respect.

Above: two Tuareg tribesmen of Ghāt, drawn in 1821 by George Lyon. These fierce warriors used to roam across the Sahara. The possibility of attack by Tuareg nomads was one of the greatest hazards facing travelers crossing the desert to Timbuktu.

less, his book *The Tuareg of the North* remains a standard work.

Early in 1869, 10 years after Duveyrier had set out to study the Tuareg, a young Dutchwoman called Alexandrine Tinné reached Marzūq with a large caravan, and a bodyguard of two Dutch sailors. Miss Tinné was a wealthy heiress, who had already spent some years in Africa, exploring in the Bahr el Ghazal region, in Algeria, and in Tunisia. Now she planned to cross the Sahara.

Soon after leaving Marzūq, Miss Tinné fell in with an Ahaggar

PORTRET van ALEXANDRINE TINNE
1835 - 1869

Tuareg chieftain, who persuaded her to let him escort her to the Oasis of Ghāt. After a few days, she was attacked by the chieftain and his Tuareg. Her hand was slashed off, probably to prevent her from drawing a revolver, and she was left lying in the hot sun to bleed slowly to death. Knowing the hazards of desert travel, Miss Tinné had taken two water tanks with her. It seems probable that her escort believed they were full of gold, and murdered her to steal them. The Sahara had claimed another victim.

Above: Alexandrine Tinné, the rich young Dutchwoman who used her fortune to finance her expeditions. She traveled lavishly, carrying curtains, cushion covers, and a small library as part of her equipment. On her last expedition, she was killed by the Tuareg.

The Desert Tamed

12

On April 4, 1881, a handful of survivors from a French expedition to the Sahara crawled into the oasis of El Meseggem. They were half-dead from thirst, hunger, and exposure. Some were badly wounded. When they had recovered, they gave a horrifying account of their journey. They had set out from Ouargla in December, 1880, the strongest military expedition that France had ever sent deep into the desert—10 officers, 46 soldiers, and 36 tribesmen. Their aim was to explore and survey the desert northeast of the Ahaggar Mountains. But this was the land of the hostile Ahaggar Tuareg who particularly disliked the French.

Scarcity of water was a great problem because of the large number of men and camels. It was this need for water that provided the Tuareg with the perfect trap. A band of tribesmen who were shadowing the expedition approached the French commander, Colonel Paul-Xavier Flatters. They told him that they would take him to a well where the camels could be watered and from which he could take a supply back to the main camp. Flatters, with a small party and most of the camels, went with them. He left a Lieutenant Dianous behind in charge of the main party.

At the well, a band of Tuareg swooped down on Flatters and his men. They shot and killed everyone except for a few Arab camel men who fled back to the camp. When Dianous heard what had

Left: one of the French Saharan regiments. The officer on horseback is the colonel of the regiment. It was this rank that Flatters held on the catastrophic mission to explore and survey the desert northeast of the Ahaggar Mountains.

Right: Paul-Xavier Flatters (1832–1881). Flatters made the fatal mistake of allowing his party to be split, and the Tuareg killed them almost to a man.

Above: an early photograph of the Foureau-Lamy mission. Their expedition across the desert proved that it was possible for a well-armed force to challenge the fierce Tuareg tribesmen in their own territory.

happened, he was faced with the terrifying task of returning to Ouargla with the survivors. They would have to walk because the Tuareg had driven away the few remaining camels.

All the way back across the desert the wretched, exhausted Frenchmen were hounded by the Tuareg. Dianous was killed, and most of the men died on the way of wounds, thirst, or starvation. When food and water had run out, the demented survivors resorted to eating the bodies of their dead companions.

The story of the disastrous Flatters expedition had an overwhelming effect on French morale. The French government had planned to build a railroad across the Sahara. Now they gave up the idea and concentrated instead upon establishing control over the areas around the desert. Tunisia became a French protectorate in 1881. In 1895, the area around Timbuktu, including much of what is now Mali, became the French colony of Sudan.

But during this period one man still dreamed of establishing a definite link across the Sahara. His name was Fernand Foureau. Between 1868 and 1898, Foureau made numerous journeys into the Sahara on his own. Altogether he covered more than 12,000 miles over the desert in preparation for the day when the French government would once again sponsor an official expedition.

Foureau's chance came in 1898. In that year the French Geographical Society, which had heard of his achievements, offered him financial backing if he would lead an expedition to explore the Sahara between Algeria and the Sudan. Foureau jumped at the opportunity. A military escort was provided under the command of a Major Lamy. Soon the expedition grew until it was more like a small army. The soldiers were armed with rifles, machine guns, and light cannon. The French government was determined that this time the Tuareg would attack at their own peril.

At last the expedition set out. The long column made its way slowly southward to the central plateau and the fearsome Ahaggar Mountains. The Tuareg, armed with swords and spears and occasionally rifles, never attacked the French. They used a more subtle way of terrorizing them. They refused to supply food or water for the camels. As the Frenchmen pushed on through the territory between the Tassili-n-Ajjer and Ahaggar Mountains, they were losing over 100 camels a week.

By the time the French had got halfway across the Aïr Mountains, all the camels were dead. Most of the luggage had to be burned, and the bulk of the ammunition buried. The men continued their march, many of them by now in rags and almost starving. At last they struggled into Zinder. The march between Algeria and the Sudan was accomplished, but their trials were not yet over. The expedition moved eastward to Lake Chad where they were attacked by an army from the kingdom of Bornu. The French managed to win the battle at Kousseri, which was renamed Fort-Lamy in memory of Major Lamy who was killed in the battle.

The Foureau-Lamy mission showed that a well-armed force of men could cross the desert. But it had not managed to overcome the Tuareg. By the end of the 1800's, the French still had no real control over their Saharan possessions or the desert tribes. They persisted in their belief that an army could subdue the tribesmen. In 1901, however, a French officer was put in charge of the Sahara who knew how to pacify the angry Tuareg and achieve the linking up of Algeria with the French Sudan.

Above: disk-lipped women of Kyabe, Chad. A traditional method of the people living near Fort-Lamy for enhancing the beauty of their women, the practice has now been forbidden. Only a handful of these women can still be found in the area.

Below: the Foureau-Lamy mission, crossing the Sahara in 1899.

Right: between 1859 and 1900, a number of Europeans set out into the Sahara, either to explore the desert, or to study the Tuareg tribesmen who lived there. This map shows the routes followed during this time by some of those who, by their journeys, helped to open up the desert.

Below: a Tuareg caravan. It was by enlisting rival desert tribesmen that the French finally succeeded in curbing the power of the Tuareg nomads.

ATLANTIC OCEAN

Essaouira (Mogador)

CANARY IS.

TROPIC OF CANCER

6b

Dakar

Senegal

Niger

Freetown

6b

.... Duveyrier	1	1859-61
—— Rohlfs	2a	1862
	2b	1863
	2c	1865
	2d	1867-8
	2e	1869
	2f	1874
	2g	1878
	2h	1880-1
— — — Nachtigal	3	1869-74
.... Lenz	4a	1879-80
	4b	1885-7
—— Flatters	5a	1880
Flatters (with Dianous)	5b	1880-1
—— Foureau	6a	1895-6
Foureau (part with Lamy)	6b	1898-19..

© Geographical Projects

This man was Marie Joseph François Henri Laperrine. When he was sent out to be commander in chief of the Saharan Oases, his job was merely to patrol the Saharan bases. But he had the ingenious idea of recruiting a force of desert tribesmen who were traditional enemies of the Tuareg. He formed them into three large camel companies. These were to be well trained and supplied with arms and food. After a number of successful brushes with the Tuareg, the camel corps began crossing the desert without fear of attack.

In May, 1902, a battle took place which finally broke the strength of the Ahaggar Tuareg. Early that year, a heavily armed French expedition had opened fire on some tribesmen who were determined to prevent them from approaching In Salah, the traditional meeting place of their chiefs. The Tuareg responded by their very effective practice of attacking French caravans traveling in their territory. The French, and their corps of desert tribesmen, took up arms against the Ahaggar Tuareg. At the Battle of Tit, in the Ahaggar Mountains, the Tuareg were heavily defeated.

Laperrine's camel corps, each usually made up of about 20 riders, continued their journeys across the Sahara. Within a few years, they hardly ever had to fire a shot. Their regular crossings of the desert paved the way for better communications. By 1910 a

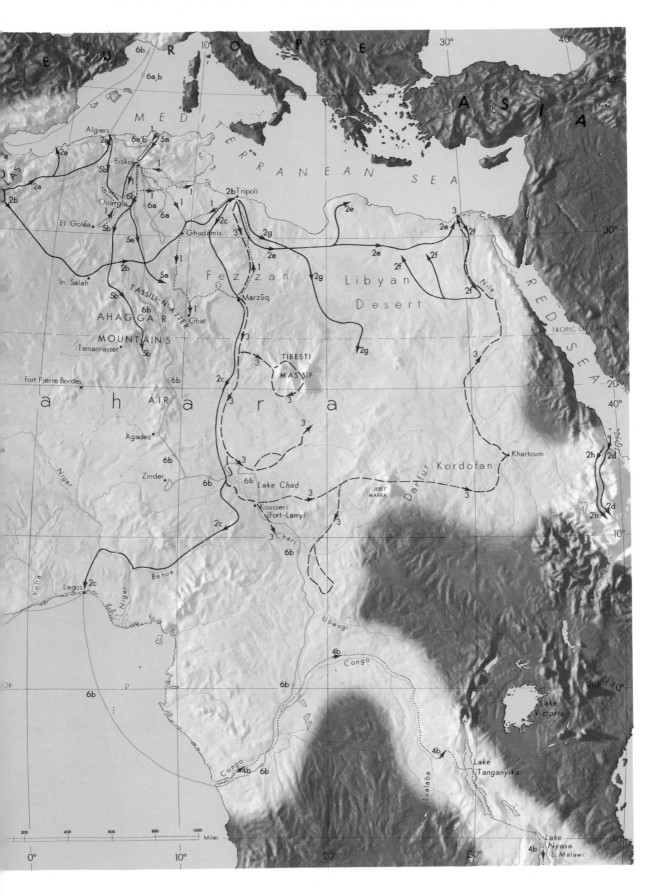

regular postal service operated across the Sahara from Timbuktu via the Ahaggar Mountains, In Salah, and El Goléa to Algiers.

Laperrine had adopted the desert way of life and had built on desert customs and rivalries in order to achieve his success. He transformed the French officers of the camel corps into a band of desert nomads. They had no headquarters, but lived with their camels wherever there was pastureland. By 1905, one of Laperrine's small groups had crossed the desert four times in the hottest season of the year without losing a single man or camel—a truly remarkable feat considering how many had died in attempting one crossing.

Ironically, Laperrine, who did so much to bring the Sahara under control, died there. In 1920, he was a passenger in one of two airplanes on an official mission to establish an air route across the Sahara from Algiers to Dakar. Somewhere near Fort Pierre Bordes, the plane Laperrine was traveling in ran out of fuel, and was forced to crash-land in the desert. The plane turned over as it struck the ground, and the general's shoulder was badly injured. The temperature in the desert was over 100°F and they had only a small supply of water. The three survivors managed to keep alive for several weeks, hoping that someone would find them. Eventually, Laperrine crawled away from the wreckage of the plane and died in the sand. Ten days later, a party of the camel corps found the general's body and the two half-dead survivors.

Unlike other parts of Africa, the work of missionaries played only a small part in the opening up of the Sahara. One reason was that the Moslem religion was well established there, and the Moslem tribesmen did not take kindly to Christian intruders. Cardinal Lavigerie, a Roman Catholic prelate, aimed to create a network of mission stations in the desert oases through the missionary White Fathers. But one group of three was murdered in 1876, and 6 years later 3 more missionaries met their deaths. Both groups had felt that they were in no danger, and it is difficult to know whether they were killed as infidel, or for the money they were carrying.

One priest who did manage to live peaceably among the Tuareg was Father Charles de Foucauld, once a classmate of Laperrine's at military school in France. Instead of going into the Saharan army De Foucauld decided to explore Morocco. There he became increasingly interested in the life of the nomadic tribesmen. Finally he decided to live the life of a monk in the Sahara. He built himself a hermitage at Tamanrasset in the heart of the Ahaggar Tuareg country, and settled down to a life devoted to prayer and the study of the desert tribesmen. He learned their language, translated their poetry, and compiled a dictionary of Tuareg words. His only difficulty in dealing with the Tuareg was that he was also a friend of the French soldiers in the Sahara, who were committed to the idea of controlling the Tuareg through French military might.

During World War I, the Turks encouraged Tuareg tribesmen to join in a "holy war" against the French posts in the desert. Although De Foucauld's hermitage at Tamanrasset seemed impregnable, it

Above: Marie Joseph Francois Henri Laperrine, who trained and armed the desert tribesmen. The camel corps he formed put an end to the absolute control the Tuareg had maintained over their desert territory.
Below: Father Charles de Foucauld, who chose to live an austere life in the desert, among the Tuareg tribesmen.

was attacked one evening and De Foucauld was shot by a band of angry nomads. In Europe he was mourned as a Christian martyr.

The murder of Charles de Foucauld marks the end of an era in Saharan exploration. World War I brought the automobile and the airplane to the Sahara—machines which were to further the conquest of the desert and foreshadow the disappearance of the camel caravan. The 1920 flight in which General Laperrine had taken part had included two primitive planes, the second one piloted by a Major Vuillemin, who did manage to complete the trip. Although Vuillemin's achievement was overshadowed by the death of the general in the desert, his crossing represented the first triumph of the machine age in northern Africa.

The first crossing of the Sahara in an automobile took place some two years later. A group of French Citroën tracked vehicles left the Mediterranean coast in December, 1922, and arrived in Timbuktu one month later. It had taken Alexander Laing 11 months to do the same crossing, and even a fast camel caravan could not manage it in less than six months. The success of the Citroën mission convinced the French that they had really conquered the desert.

By this time, the exploration of the Sahara was no longer simply a question of overcoming the difficulties of climate and terrain. The desert's fascinating history was to occupy the next generation of adventurers. In 1933, a French officer, Lieutenant Brenans, discovered carvings of human figures and animals on the walls of

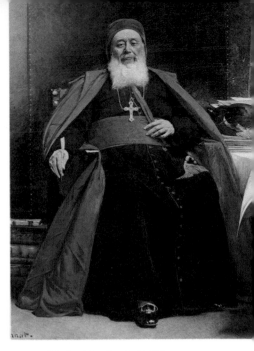

Above: Cardinal Lavigerie (1825–1892). He founded the White Fathers, a Roman Catholic order of priests who went to the Sahara to seek converts. His portrait now hangs in Versailles. Below: a White Father talking to a group of local children. Behind them is a typical example of the buildings of the area, constructed of dried mud.

RAID·CITROËN
MISSION
G^{LE}·M·HAARDT·E·L·AUDOUIN·DUBREUIL

PARTIE·DE·TOUGGOURT·UNE·MISSION·ORGANISÉE·PAR·A·^{DRE}·CITROËN
ARRIVE·A·TOMBOUCTOU·AYANT·POUR·LA·PREMIERE·FOIS
EN·AUTOMOBILE·FRANCHI·LE·DESERT·DU·SAHARA
7·DECEMBRE·1922——7·JANVIER·1923

Above: a plaque commemorating the Citroën expedition over the Sahara, which consisted of five caterpillar-wheeled Citroën cars. They arrived at Timbuktu on January 7, 1923, having taken only a month on their journey.

a rocky gorge in the Tassili-n-Ajjer. In the caverns beneath the walls of the gorge he found rock paintings. These amazing works of art were subsequently examined by scholars and established as part of the Sahara's prehistoric culture. The rock paintings showed the different races of men which had once lived in the Sahara, and the different kinds of animals which had roamed there. Most important were the clues the paintings gave about the desert's climate. There were pictures of elephants, some blowing water out of their trunks, rhinoceroses, hippopotamuses—all animals which live in tropical regions rather than in deserts. Archaeologists, speculating on the age of the Sahara, used the evidence of the cave paintings to support their theory that about 40,000 years ago the Sahara was a tropical region with rivers, lakes, and swamps.

Alongside the investigation of the history and art of the Sahara, other vitally important exploration was being carried out in the desert. In the 1930's, scientists were already predicting that large deposits of oil, gas, and minerals existed under the desert. It was

Right: the customs of centuries and the present-day world rub shoulders in North Africa today. Here a woman dressed as her great-grandmother would have dressed takes her child in a modern pushchair past a modern truck.

Below: the countries of northern Africa and the Arabian Peninsula in 1970. As the European explorers spread into Africa, they took with them the influence of European culture and civilization. Gradually almost the entire continent was brought under European rule. After World War II, however, a move toward self-government began in Africa, and by 1970 almost all the African countries had gained independence.

not until after World War II, however, that oil companies from the United States, France, and Britain began to drill for oil. Within about a year (1955–1956), enough oil fields were found to establish the Sahara as one of the major oil-producing areas of the world.

The period after World War II was also a time of political change. From 1922, the Sahara had remained largely under French control. But by the 1950's Africa was changing from a continent of European-ruled colonies to one of self-governing countries. Morocco and Tunisia became independent countries in 1956, while Algeria gained her independence in 1962 after a long and bitter war.

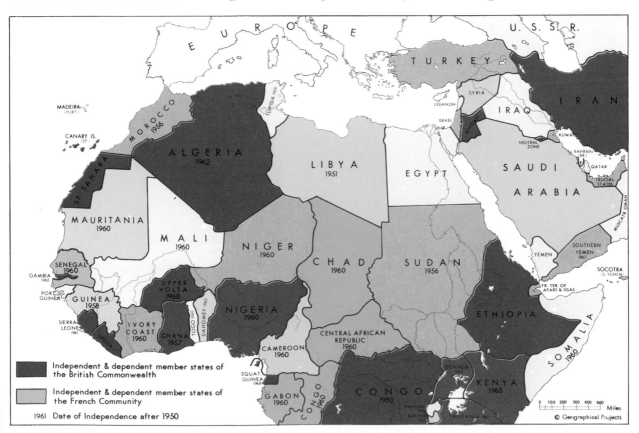

Above: the empty wastes of the Sahara, for so long thought to be valueless, are at last revealing their hidden wealth. Under the sand lie vast deposits of minerals and oil, and it is on these that the future of the desert rests. Here, an oil jet flames against the desert sky, symbolizing the challenge modern technology presents to the people of the area.

The courage and determination of the early explorers in the face of overwhelming odds helped to conquer the great "seas of sand." But what started as an exploration of unknown and mysterious regions will continue in other ways. The Sahara, with its vast hidden resources, and its great development potential, is now on the threshold of an exciting future. Further exploration in the desert will involve businessmen, politicians, scientists, technicians, and engineers. Together, they will devise new schemes for developing this rich area. Their achievements will yield further secrets to a scientific and technological age. The story has not yet ended.

Right: death was a frequent companion on early expeditions. Here Richard Lander buries his master, Hugh Clapperton.

Appendix

The exploration of the determined men in this book has a curiously modern flavor. Part of this is undoubtedly because much of the exploration has been relatively recent, but there remains the haunting circumstance that much of the land over which the explorers rode and plodded would look much the same to them if they returned today. The vastness of the Sahara and the Arabian deserts, the inaccessibility of the Niger region, have helped to sustain the pattern of life—or the waste of emptiness—that has continued from time immemorial.

For these reasons the selections in this appendix vary from descriptions of people and places long vanished, like the Mamelukes that Di Varthema joined in the 1500's, to discussions of problems still very relevant to the emerging Arab world, such as the place of women in Arab society. The outsiders who found the scenes of this book sources of a special fascination were most often intriguing people in their own right, and the excerpts from their writings show a glimpse of the places they saw through the filter of their own personalities. Both the "problem of the Niger" and the desert exerted an irresistible attraction to the European world of the 1800's, and the men who left that comfortable world for the unknown hardships and treacheries of Africa and Arabia often paid dearly for yielding to that fascination. The desert and the river could be cruel, and of the many that went out, few returned.

Following this group of original documents there is a brief biographical dictionary of the most important explorers and travelers covered in *Seas of Sand*. In many cases, maps of the routes followed by the explorers accompany the biographies.

After the biographies, there is a glossary which gives the meaning of the many unfamiliar words and phrases used in the text. An index and a list of picture credits completes the book.

The Mamelukes of Damascus

Above: a woodcut from an early edition of Di Varthema's book about his adventures, showing some Mameluke guards accosting a townsman.

Above: a Mameluke exercising his horse, as seen in Egypt in 1801. By 1801, the Mamelukes were no longer the rulers of Egypt.

Ludovico di Varthema never says when the idea of disguising himself as a Mameluke for the pilgrimage to Mecca first occurred to him—a pity, as it was a flash of inspiration. The Mamelukes, many of them recruited from Christian prisoners of war who were willing to embrace Islam, were the elite guard which ruled much of the Middle East of his time. In this passage from his travels Di Varthema describes how he joined the Mamelukes at Damascus.

"Truly it would not be possible to describe the beauty and the excellence of this Damascus, in which I resided some months in order to learn the Moorish language, because this city is entirely inhabited by Moors and Mamelukes and many Greek Christians. . . . . You must know that in the city of Damascus there is a very beautiful and strong castle, which is said to have been built by a Florentine Mameluke at his own expense, he being lord of the said city. . . . Fifty Mamelukes, in the service of the Grand Sultan, are constantly quartered with the governor of the castle. . . .

"The Mamelukes are renegade Christians, who have been purchased. Certain it is that the said Mamelukes never lose any time, but are constantly exercising themselves either in arms or in letters,

Above: one of the sights on the way to Mecca was the supernatural light traditionally believed to shine over the tomb of the Prophet Mohammed.

in order that they may acquire excellence. And you must know that every Mameluke, great or little, has for his pay six saraphi per month, and his expenses for himself, his horse, and a family; and they have as much more when they are engaged on any warlike expedition. The said Mamelukes, when they go about the city, are always in companies of two or three, as it would be a great disgrace if they went alone. . . . When a Moor meets a Mameluke, although he be the principal merchant of the place, he is obliged to do honour and give place to the Mameluke, and if he do not so he is punished.

"In 1503, on the 8th day of April, the caravan being set in order to go to Mecca, and I being desirous of beholding various scenes and not knowing how to set about it, formed a great friendship with the captain of the said Mamelukes of the caravan, who was a Christian renegade, so that he clothed me like a Mameluke and gave me a good horse, and placed me in company with the other Mamelukes, and this was accomplished by means of the money and other things which I gave him; and in this manner we set ourselves on the way."

The Travels of Ludivico di Varthema, *trans. by John Winter Jones (Hakluyt Society: London, 1863) pp. 8-9, 13, 16.*

The City that Used to Be

Desert cities live ephemeral lives. When Aden was occupied by the British in 1839, it drew trade away from the nearby coffee-exporting center, Al Mukhá. Since that time, the desert sands have gradually encroached upon Al Mukhá, its population has moved away, and its buildings have decayed. Here is a traveler's report of Al Mukhá in its prime.

"On landing at a pier, which has been constructed for the convenience of trade, the effect is improved by the battlements of the walls, and a lofty tower on which cannon are mounted, which advances before the town, and is meant to protect the sea gate. The moment, however, that the traveller passes the gates, these pleasing ideas are put to flight by the filth that abounds in every street, and more particularly, in the open spaces which are left within the walls, by the gradual decay of the deserted habitations which once filled them. The principal building in the town is the residence of the dola, which is large and lofty, having one front to the sea, and another to a square. Another side of the square, which is the only regular place in the town, is filled up by the official residence of the *bas ketab,* or secretary of state. These buildings externally have no pretensions to

architectural elegance, yet are by no means ugly objects, from their turretted tops, and fantastic ornaments in white stucco. The windows are in general small, stuck into the wall in an irregular manner, closed with lattices, and sometimes opening into a wooden, carved-wood balcony. In the upper apartments, there is generally a range of circular windows above the others, filled with a thin strata of transparent stone. None of these can be opened, and only a few of the lower ones, in consequence of which, a thorough air is rare in their houses; yet, the people of rank do not seem oppressed

Left: the mosque in Al Mukhā, now only a shell. As the desert sand encroaches farther into the town, it has lost its former prosperity, and today it is dying.

Right: coffee drinkers in Al Mukhā. Once a proud and flourishing city, all that now remains famous is the English version of its name. Mocha today means a variety of coffee.

Below left: the desert winds are always blowing sand into the towns and only the rush of people keeps the streets clear. But in Al Mukhā most of the people have gone.

by the heat, which is frequently almost insupportable to a European. As they never use a level, the floors are extremely uneven; but this is a trifling inconvenience to people who never use chairs or tables, but are always reclining on couches, supported on every side by cushions. The internal construction of their houses is uniformly bad. Little lime is used in any of their buildings; constant care is therefore necessary to prevent the introduction of moisture; but, with caution, they last for many years. If, however, a house is neglected, it speedily becomes a heap of rubbish; the walls returning to their original state of mud, from which they had been formed into bricks by the heat of the sun alone. The wooden materials very soon vanish in a country where firing is extremely scarce, so that even the ruins of cities which were celebrated for their magnificence in former times, may now be sought for in vain."

The Modern Traveller, A Description, Geographical, Historical and Topographical, of the Various Countries of the Globe, Vol. IV, *Josian Condor (James Duncan: London, 1830) pp. 314-315.*

Women in Arab Society

Above: a girl from Yemen, from an engraving by Baurenfeind brought back by Niebuhr. As for centuries, the slave girls then went unveiled.

Below: the alabaster head of an Arab woman, from the century before Christ, excavated by Wendell Phillips in Oman.

Arab women have always been kept in a greatly subordinate position in their society, and one of the main problems of the Arab countries in coming to terms with today's world has been how to open horizons for their women. This extract is by an American, Wendell Phillips, who has done a great deal of archaeological work in Oman and has become familiar with the society of that Arabian state.

"In terms of personality, of economics, of politics and of civics, there are no women in Oman; women exist in number always greater than men, but their existence is domestic and servile only. The unequal position of women in Oman is common throughout the Arabian peninsula; the attitude which degrades them is common to the whole Arab world and beyond that to the whole Muslim world; but the worst practices, the excesses of the system, are being abandoned in the more sophisticated Muslim states and are confined now to the poverty-stricken parts of the Arabian peninsula itself. Moreover, and curiously enough, the existence of a desert woman may be less oppressive, freer, than that of her urban sister, if only because of the greater need for her active services in the work of the community. . . .

"There is no future but marriage for any woman of Oman at the present time. Doubtless economic changes will make a difference there, as elsewhere; but it should be remembered that the Arabs believe that 'a woman's lot is a husband or else the grave.' It was not always so; there is evidence that women in Arabia generally were more free and more respected as full human beings, in their own right, in pre-Islamic times. . . .

"Although Mohammed once said, 'Paradise is at the feet of mothers,' it is an accepted fact that depending on their social status, with rare exceptions, Arab women are the downtrodden, mindless slaves of their fathers, brothers, and husbands, who rule them like tyrants. They bear the babies, carry the loads, cook the food, and eat what their men leave behind. The dirty and disagreeable tasks fall to them. This is as true among Bedouin today as ever it was. Whether high born or low, the Bedouin women, even if they have slaves, are all obliged to put up and prepare the tents, to strike and roll them up, and to load and unload them, as is needed; also to attend to all the domestic work, such as collecting wood and dung to cook on; and

lastly to find time as best they can to look after and bring up their children. By twenty-eight the majority are old and worn-out grandmothers, sorrowfully facing an early death from day to day without the slightest security from the ever-present menace of dislodgment through divorce, the indoor sport of Arabia.

"The problem of the status of women, which has steadily declined, places the sincere Muslim reformer in his most embarrassing dilemma; but the feeling against polygamy (wives are an expensive hobby, for a wife means new clothes) is becoming a strong social conviction throughout this 'civilized' twentieth-century world. In all fairness to Mohammed, it must be said that he limited polygamy rather than introduced the practice among the Arabs. . . .

"Although Mohammed was responsible for putting down the practice of female infanticide, he adopted a method by which all females could be immured for ever in a living grave, by the institution of the *burqa,* the veil. The veil was probably unknown in Oman before Islam. . . .

"Were I a woman in Oman I personally would infinitely prefer to be a slave girl than a 'free' Arab woman, even though she is usually placid, like a well-fed cow. As opposed to a helpless and hopeless, closely-veiled lifetime of rigid physical and moral confinement, sinking in the sloth of ignorance and eclipse, the unimprisoned slave girl is relatively free, for she walks unveiled, where she pleases, with whom she pleases."

Unknown Oman *Wendell Phillips (Longmans: London, 1966) pp. 128-129, 140-141, 144.*

Above: a bride in Muscat awaiting the arrival of her husband, whom she has never seen. Her palms, fingernails, and toenails are decorated with henna, a dark reddish-orange dye.

Right: an Omani woman brings her sick child to a foreign clinic. She is shown wearing the *burqa,* the traditional veil.

The Wahhabis Rise Again

The changeless pattern of tribal life in the Arabian desert presented great difficulties to Abdul Aziz ibn Saud when in the early 1900's he began a campaign to raise the banner of a new Wahhabism over a united Arabia. In this passage, St. John Philby, who was later his adviser, describes the complex situation Ibn Saud found himself in. In particular he outlines Ibn Saud's reasons for undertaking major reforms of the whole fabric of desert society.

"Internally, Ibn Sa'ud was confronted by a problem. Arabia was essentially a country of nomad tribes with a highly developed sense of tribal solidarity accompanied by an intense individualism which promised ill for any attempt to weld the centrifugal elements of its population into a national, much less imperial, whole. History had already proved that such an objective was eminently feasible

Above: Abdul Aziz ibn Saud in his camp in 1911, during the Wahhabi resurgence. The photograph was taken by a British officer there at the time.

Below: a Wahhabi raiding party in 1911, carrying the standard of Ibn Saud across the desert as their fore-runners did over 100 years before.

under certain conditions, but that, those conditions being essentially evanescent in the social climate of Arabia, it could not be maintained indefinitely. No permanent political structure could be raised on the shifting sands of nomad society, which faithfully reflected the physical conditions of the country in which it had developed through hundreds and even thousands of years. The problem thus posed by the unchangeable natural conditions of the country was therefore insoluble, and Ibn Sa'ud set himself the task of solving it.

"From the history of the rise and fall of the old Wahhabi Empire he culled the lesson that the innate fanaticism of a desert people could be stirred under the influence of a great idea to galvanise its dissident elements into common action in a common cause, and that such a cause could be maintained so long as the great idea remained actively operative and the fanaticism was kept at white heat. Like a forest fire it would burn unconquerably as long as there was fuel to feed it; and in this case the fuel was constant aggression and expansion at the expense of those who did not share the great idea. There was obviously some natural limit to such a process, and when that limit was reached, as it had been at the beginning of the nineteenth century with the conquest of all Arabia, the fire would have to feed on itself and so gradually die out, even if there was no one to hasten the process with water and earth. The tribal elements of the Wahhabi army would tend to disintegrate and quarrel, becoming an easy prey to any invader and a certain cause of internal disruption. This is what actually happened with amazing suddenness at the moment when the Wahhabi power seemed to be at its zenith. The Turks appeared; there was no more left for the tribesmen to loot who had already looted everything; war without the prospect of loot was unattractive; on the other hand, the gifts that poured into the country with the forces of Muhammed 'Ali were more than welcome; and those would get them who claimed them first; and, finally, man had triumphantly vindicated God's cause, and it was surely now for God to defend it against the evil-doers. The tribal conscience was easily salved, and the tribes hastened to make the best terms, each for itself. The general cause went by the board. . . .

"It was abundantly clear that no permanent structure could ever be built on Badawin foundations; and there can be no doubt whatever that Ibn Sa'ud, in the course of his musings, deliberately formulated this conclusion as to the conditions which governed his ambitions, and equally deliberately envisaged and adopted the only logical alternative. And that was nothing less than to uproot and destroy the very foundations of Badawin society, which had endured without the slightest change since the days of Abraham and Isaac and Jacob, and to replace them with the concrete of a national spirit on which to build up an Arabian nation."

Arabia *H. St. J. B. Philby (Ernest Benn: London, 1930) pp. 180-181, 183.*

The Forbidden City

Like all ceremonies restricted to believers, the rites at Mecca have had a peculiar fascination for outsiders. Naturally for many of the explorers who reached the sacred city, the mere fact of being in and describing Mecca itself seemed enough. But the pilgrimage which they managed to share has for centuries been a most significant and meaningful religious experience for millions of Moslems. What do the ceremonies mean to them? This extract, taken from a modern account of the pilgrimage, explains its traditional significance, and in particular the tawaf, or ceremonial circling of the Kaaba.

Above: the rock near Mecca where it is believed that Mohammed used to retire to meditate in peace, sitting beneath it in the cool and private shade.

Right: the great prayer outside the town wall of Mecca, at the end of an important festival. All the backs bend in the direction of the sacred Kaaba.

Below: the Kaaba, the Cubical House, viewed from Mount Keyis, in a photograph taken in 1901. Outside the times of pilgrimage, Mecca is a quiet city.

"According to Mohammedan tradition, in 1892 B.C. God ordered Abraham to emigrate with his son, Ismail, and Ismail's mother, Hagar, to this valley. . . . Here Hagar lived with her son and built herself a house, the Patriarch coming from Palestine to visit her from time to time. He was then ordered by God to make of this house a temple where people prayed; he, therefore, demolished it and built the Cubical House [the Kaaba] on its site. Mecca, according to an Arab authority, is the Babylonian word for house. . . .

"The Mohammedan law prescribes for every pilgrim the washing, if possible, of the whole body before entering Mecca. The pilgrim passes through several roads and visits a number of tombs, such as those of the first wife of Mohammed and the first to believe in his mission, his mother, his grandfathers, and others, before reaching the Haram, or precincts of the Cubical House. . . . The pilgrim then directs his steps to the door of Shiba which is composed of two pillars surmounted by an arch through which he passes, and offers up a prayer. He then proceeds to the south side of the Kaaba, thence to the Hagar Al-Asward, or the Black Stone, praying the whole time. The Haram stands in the middle of Mecca. . . . Its angles are not right angles and in its four corners domes are built. . . . It has an un-roofed courtyard, intersected with many alleys, in the middle of which rises the Kaaba, to the east of which stands the tomb of Abraham. . . .

"The black stone is situated outside the Kaaba at its southern angle. It is oval in shape and is black but somewhat reddish in colour. . . . It is placed in a silver case with a circular aperture. At this aperture the stone has become concave like a native drinking-bowl from the touch of the millions of pilgrims. This stone, according

to Mohammedan tradition, fell to the earth from some star. . . . It is absurd, say the Mohammedan authorities, to allege that the Moslems worship this stone. . . . It is to be looked upon like the flags of nations which are respected, not because they are pieces of canvas hung on poles, but because they are the emblems of the king's might and power. . . . The struggle among the pilgrims to kiss this stone is indescribable. Those who are at some distance of it do not hesitate to push and even strike those who are nearer the stone in order to get them out of their way, and when this manner of approaching the stone is in vain they mount on the shoulders of others and thus get to it. . . .

"The Kaaba became the Kibla, or the point towards which Mohammedans all over the world look in prayer, in the second year of the Hegira. Previous to that year Mohammedans turned their faces to Jerusalem while praying.

"As soon as the pilgrim reaches the Sacred City he begins the tawaf, or walking around the Kaaba seven times. One of the principal conditions of the tawaf is perfect purity, the pilgrim not being allowed to carry in his hand his shoes or anything unclean. The tawaf begins from the Black Stone, which the pilgrim should touch

The Forbidden City

and, if possible, kiss. The pilgrim makes this journey at least once after every one of five prayers. Some, however, cover this distance before and after each prayer, while Indians and Javanese, worn out with years or with disease, go to Mecca in the hope of dying during the tawaf which they perform on a stretcher carried by four men. They consider death in the sacred precincts of the Kaaba as the greatest happiness of their lives. . . .

"The idea of wearing the ihram dress is, according to Moslem authorities, because it was the simple dress said to have been worn by Abraham; further, it is a sign that the faithful has discarded the luxuries of this world and gone back to the primitive condition of man, in which the rich and the poor were alike, to the first dress of man on coming to the world and his last on leaving it. . . .

"After the pilgrim has performed all the prescribed visits to the holy places of Mecca, he goes, still in his dress of the ihram, to Arafat. After a total march of six hours from Mecca the pilgrims reach the mountain of Arafat, which is a level ground surrounded by mountains, close to a hill of pebbles called the Mountain of Mercy or, more commonly, the Mountain of Arafat. It is called by this name because Adam is said to have made the acquaintance of Eve at this place, or because the Archangel Gabriel said to Abraham there: 'Confess thy sins and learn the rites of my religion.' Pilgrimage becomes fully accomplished only when the Moslem has stood there."

The Moslem Pilgrimage *S. Spiro Bey* (*Whitehead Morris Limited: Alexandria, 1932*) *pp. 35, 36-37, 40-41, 42, 45, 46-47.*

Below: the pilgrims arrive at Mount Arafat, the last holy place they must visit to complete the pilgrimage.

Captured by the Moors

Above: Mungo Park, one of the most famous of the African explorers, who died in his attempt to follow the Niger down to its mouth at the sea.

Mungo Park was a determined and resourceful man. With no disguise, no knowledge of local languages, and no experience of exploration, he plunged into the African interior. Robbed of his possessions, he was taken prisoner by a group of "Moors", apparently Moslems of the Mali area. This account, taken from his Life and Travels, describes his first meeting with their king, an old man named Ali, and the treatment he received among the Moors who had captured him.

"About five o'clock we came in sight of Benown, the residence of Ali. It presented to the eye a great number of dirty-looking tents, scattered without order over a large space of ground; and among the tents appeared large herds of camels, cattle, and goats. We reached the skirts of this camp a little before sunset, and with much entreaty, procured a little water. My arrival was no sooner observed, than the people who drew water at the wells threw down their buckets; those in the tents mounted their horses; and men, women, and children, came running or galloping towards me. I soon found myself surrounded by such a crowd that I could scarcely move; one pulled my clothes, another took off my hat, a third stopped me to examine my waistcoat buttons, and a fourth called out, *La illah el Allah Mahamet rasowl allahi*—('There is but one God, and Moham-

Below: a party of slaves being herded to market. Like many explorers, Mungo Park found himself dependent on slavers, despite his hatred of their trade.

Captured by the Moors

Left: Mungo Park apparently found the curiosity of the local people about his color and clothing disconcerting.

Below: Mungo Park spending the night in the hut of a woman and her female relatives, who had taken pity on him after his flight from the Moors.

med is his prophet')—and signified, in a threatening manner, that I must repeat these words. We reached at length the king's tent, where we found a great number of people, men and women, assembled. Ali was sitting upon a black leather cushion, clipping a few hairs from his upper lip; a female attendant holding up a looking-glass before him. He appeared to be an old man, of the Arab cast, with a long white beard; and he had a sullen and indignant aspect. He surveyed me with attention, and inquired of the Moors if I could speak Arabic; being answered in the negative, he appeared much surprised, and continued silent. The surrounding attendants, and especially the ladies, were abundantly more inquisitive; they asked a thousand questions, inspected every part of my apparel, searched my pockets, and obliged me to unbutton my waistcoat, and display the whiteness of my skin; they even counted my toes and fingers, as if they doubted whether I was in truth a human being. In a little time the priest announced evening prayers; but before the people departed, the Moor who had acted as interpreter, informed me that

Ali was about to present me with something to eat; and looking round, I observed some boys bringing a wild hog, which they tied to one of the tent strings, and Ali made signs to me to kill and dress it for supper. Though I was very hungry, I did not think it prudent to eat any part of an animal so much detested by the Moors, and therefore told him that I never ate such food. They then untied the hog, in hopes that it would run immediately at me—for they believe that a great enmity subsists between hogs and Christians—but in this they were disappointed; for the animal no sooner regained his liberty, than he began to attack indiscriminately every person that came in his way, and at last took shelter under the couch upon which the king was sitting. The assembly being thus dissolved, I was conducted to the tent of Ali's chief slave, but was not permitted to enter, nor allowed to touch anything belonging to it. I requested something to eat, and a little boiled corn, with salt and water, was at length sent me in a wooden bowl; and a mat was spread upon the sand before the tent, on which I passed the night, surrounded by the curious multitude."

The Life and Travels of Mungo Park (*William P. Nimmo: Edinburgh, 1870) pp. 95-97.*

Below: Park drank from a trough with the cows when an old man refused to let him drink from his bucket, which he thought Christian lips would pollute.

The Death of Clapperton

Above: Richard Lander in Arab dress. Lander was only in his early twenties when he accompanied Clapperton to Africa, but after Clapperton's death he managed to reach the coast alone.

Richard Lander was an adventurous young man from Cornwall, engaged as a "confidential servant" by Hugh Clapperton, recently returned from his first journey to Africa and at the height of his fame. Lander went to Clapperton to ask to accompany him on his next expedition. Neither man could have guessed that it would be Lander alone who returned, bringing with him the valuable notes of their discoveries. Here is his account of Clapperton's death.

"On the morning of the 13th, being awake, I was greatly alarmed on hearing a peculiar rattling noise issuing from my master's throat, and his breathing at the same time was loud and difficult. At that moment, on his calling out 'Richard!' in a low, hurried, and singular tone, I was instantly at his side, and was astonished beyond measure on beholding him sitting upright in his bed (not having been able for a long time previously to move a limb), and staring wildly around. Observing him ineffectually struggling to raise himself on his feet, I clasped him in my arms, and whilst I thus held him, could feel his heart palpitating violently. His throes became every moment less vehement, and at last they entirely

Right: an illustration from Lander's book showing a method of crossing a stream—clinging to a floating barrel.

ceased, insomuch that thinking he had fallen into a slumber, or was overpowered by faintings, I placed his head gently on my left shoulder, gazing for an instant, on his pale and altered features; some indistinct expressions quivered on his lips, and whilst he vainly strove to give them utterance, his heart ceased to vibrate, and his eyes closed for ever!

"I held the lifeless body in my arms for a short period, overwhelmed with grief; nor could I bring myself to believe that the soul which had animated it with being, a few moments before, had actually quitted it.

"I then unclasped my arms, and held the hand of my dear master in mine; but it was cold and dead, and instead of returning the warmth with which I used to press it, imparted some of its own unearthly chillness to my frame, and fell heavily from my grasp. O God! what was my distress in that agonizing moment? Shedding floods of tears, I flung myself along the bed of death, and prayed that Heaven would in mercy take my life!"

Records of Captain Clapperton's Last Expedition to Africa *Richard Lander (Henry Colburn and Richard Bentley: London, 1830) pp. 74-76.*

Below: one of Lander's most dangerous experiences on his return journey was a trial by poison to prove he was not hostile to a tribe. He survived the ordeal.

Alexandrine Tinné among the Tuareg

Everything about Alexandrine Tinné, her youth, her wealth, her attractiveness, made her a remarkable person to find in the far reaches of the barely-known world. She was clearly an interesting person as well, observing sharply and capable of writing her observations vividly. This excerpt from letters of 1869—the year of her death at the hands of the Tuareg—shows her quick sympathy with these desert tribesmen, when she met them under the protection of their chief Ichnuchen, the supreme chief of the Ajjer Tuareg.

"I cannot tell you the impression the scene of Ichnuchen in his strange stately dress, and of all his followers made on me, old travelier as I am. I never saw a grander and handsomer sight, those variegated colours, martial appearance, singular trappings, and elegant dromedaries with long snake necks.

"The Tuareg are evidently a quite different race from the Arabs, tall, powerfully-built men, without that thinness or rather slimness of the Arabs, and with nothing of that hooked nose, rather apish and anxious face. They seem to me, however, not at all to be of European origin as is said: they are too brown. They have such a

Above: an early photograph of a camel caravan crossing the desert, seen in silhouette against the horizon. The Tuareg traveled in this way for centuries across their desert domain.

Left: a Tuareg warrior dances with elegant grace in a garden courtyard.

Right: Alexandrine Tinné, the Dutch heiress who met her death in the Sahara

peculiar laugh, that once heard remains in your ears, and all our people could not help imitating them the whole day, as when one hears a new song one keeps repeating it. They have also a queer squeak they use for exciting their camels, but from force of habit introduce it into conversation also.

"Unlike Arabs they are lively, take interest in all they see, live very rough, and have none of that Oriental effeminate softness. And though their curiosity to see us was so obstreperous that we had a quarrel about it with them, it denotes to my idea, a certain

inquisitiveness of mind that would be a good quality if trained to polite proportions, and is better, not for the tourist's comfort, but for the human race, than a dull apathy.

"Their reputation of pride is also not exaggerated. They, without doing positive harm, evidently consider themselves a superior race, and treated the Arabs as a Turk would treat a fellah, as a soldier a *pays conquis* [conquered land], and bullied about the natives of the place.

"They at first were very nice with us, though rather too curious, for if we were surprised at their sight, *ils nous l'ont bien rendu* [they were just as surprised], and group after group came to wonder at my Algerian women, 'so white and so neat,' they said, but at last they became too free, and I got very angry and complained to Ichnuchen who immediately put strict order and stopped the nuisance. Ichnuchen was very civil."

Travels of Alexine *Penelope Gladstone (John Murray: London, 1970) pp. 215, 217.*

The Explorers

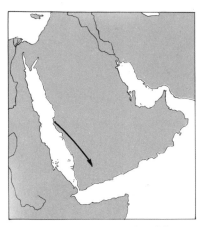

ARNAUD, JOSEPH THOMAS
1812–1884   France
1840–1841: Made two expeditions,
financed by Mehemet Ali, to the basin
of the Nile.
1843: Traveled with a Turkish party
from Juddah to the Marib dam.

BARTH, HEINRICH
1821–1865   Germany
1845–1847: Traveled overland from
Rabat to Egypt. Visited Middle Eastern
countries.
1850–1851: With a British expedition,
crossed the Sahara from Tripoli to Lake
Chad. On death of Richardson, the
expedition's leader, appointed to lead
the expedition.
1852–1855: Continued to Timbuktu.
Returned to Tripoli via the Niger,
Lake Chad, and the Sahara. Made first
reliable maps of parts of northern
Africa and studied Negro customs.
See map on page 123

BAURENFEIND, WILLIAM
(?)–1763   Germany
1761: Left Copenhagen for Arabia
with Niebuhr's scientific expedition.
1762: Arrived at Juddah. Traveled
in northern Yemen.
1763: Left Al Mukhā for Şan'ā', the
Yemenite capital. Stayed there 10 days,
then returned to Al Mukhā. On board
ship for Bombay, Baurenfeind died.
See Niebuhr map on page 64.

BELL, GERTRUDE
1868–1926   England
1899: Visited Palestine and Syria,
on the first of numerous journeys in
the Middle East.
1913: Became the second woman to
travel to Hā'il, in Arabia.
1914(?): Appointed to the Arab
intelligence bureau.
1920: Became Oriental secretary to the
High Commissioner of Iraq.
See map on page 85.

BENT, JAMES THEODORE
1852–1897   England
1885–1887: Studied local traditions
and customs in the Greek islands.
1888–1893: Undertook archaeological
research in the Middle East.
1893–1894: Led an expedition to
explore the interior of the Hadhramaut.
Visited Katan and Shibām.
1894–1895: Explored Dhofar and the
Qara Mountains. *See map on page 64.*

BLUNT, WILFRID SCAWEN
1840–1922   England
1858–1869: Member of British
diplomatic service.
1878: With his wife and a party of
Bedouins, left Damascus for the Nejd to
buy Arab horses for breeding. Traveled
to the Persian Gulf via the An Nafūd.
See map on page 85.

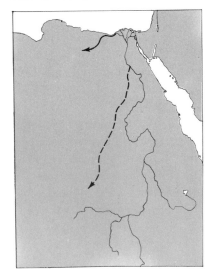

BROWNE, WILLIAM GEORGE
1768–1813   England
1792: Explored the western Egyptian
desert. Was the first European after
Alexander the Great to visit the oasis of
Siwah.
1813: Murdered near Tabriz in Persia.
See map at bottom of previous column.

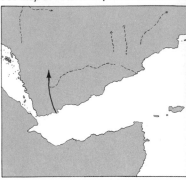

BURCHARDT, HERMANN
(?)–1909   Germany
1908(?): Traveled in southwestern
Arabia.
1909: Murdered.

BURCKHARDT, JOHN LEWIS
1784–1817   Switzerland
1806: Visited England and accepted
an offer from the Association for
Promoting the Discovery of the Interior
Parts of Africa to search for the sources
of the Niger.
1810: Disguised himself as a Turk
under the name of Ibrahim ibn Abdulla.
Studied Moslem customs and learned
Arabic.
1812: Traveled in Palestine and Syria.
1813–1815: Traveled up the Nile to
the Red Sea port of Suakin. Crossed to
Juddah and made the pilgrimage to

Mecca. Wrote an account of his
journey which became essential
reading for any traveler to the region.
1816: Returned, exhausted, to Cairo.
See map on page 64.

BURTON, SIR RICHARD FRANCIS
1821–1890   England
1842–1849: Served with the British
Army in India, where he traveled widely.
1853–1854: Made the pilgrimage to

Mecca, disguised as a Moslem holy man.
1854–1859: Traveled in Africa with John Hanning Speke. Discovered Lake Tanganyika (1858).
See map on page 64.

BURY, G. WYMAN (ABDULLA MANSUR)
1874–(?)   England
(?): Served with the British Army in Arabia. Lived with the Arabs and learned Arabic.
1908: Planned to cross Yemen and travel to the southern Nejd. Turkish opposition thwarted his plan.
1913: Spent his honeymoon in Ṣan'ā'.
1915(?): Served as intelligence officer in the Suez Canal area.

CAILLIÉ, RENÉ
1799–1838   France
1816: Joined a French ship bound for Senegal. There, joined an expedition searching for Mungo Park.
1827: Left Sierra Leone for Timbuktu. Sailed to the Rio Nunez, then joined a caravan. In August held up for five months by illness.
1828: Reached Timbuktu, the first Frenchman to do so. Crossed the Sahara Desert to Morocco. Traveled through the Grand Atlas to Tangier.
See map on page 123.

CLAPPERTON, HUGH
1788–1827   Scotland
1822–1825: With Denham and Oudney, tried to reach the Niger from

Tripoli. First Europeans to see Lake Chad. Joined a caravan for Kano but at Sokoto was prevented from continuing to the Niger.
1825–1827: With his servant, Lander, tried to reach the Niger from Badagri. Crossed the river at Bussa but was again held up at Sokoto, where he died.
See map on page 123.

DAVIDSON, JOHN
1797–1836   England
1835: Traveled as a physician in the Sultanate of Morocco.
1836: Attempted to cross the Sahara from Morocco, through Mauritania to Timbuktu. Murdered six weeks out from Morocco.

DENHAM, DIXON
1786–1828   England
1822–1825: With Clapperton and Oudney, tried to cross the Sahara to the Niger. First Europeans to see Lake Chad. Left companions to explore Chari River. Rejoined Clapperton at Kukawa and crossed the Sahara to Tripoli.
1825: Appointed superintendent of liberated Africans at Sierra Leone.
1828: Appointed lieutenant governor of Sierra Leone.
See map on page 123.

DOUGHTY, CHARLES MONTAGU
1843–1926   England
1875: Traveled to Damascus.
1876–1878: Traveled from Damascus into the Nejd. Visited Taymā', Hā'il, Buraydah, and 'Unayzah. Reached the

Red Sea port of Juddah.
1888: Published *Travels in Arabia Deserta,* the definitive work on the region.
See map on page 85.

DUVEYRIER, HENRI
1840–1892   France
1857: First visit to northern Africa.
1859: Traveled from Algeria to El Goléa in the Sahara. Visited the Tassili-n-Ajjer, and made extensive explorations of the desert. Lived as one of the Tuareg tribesmen.
1864: Published *The Tuareg of the North.*
See map on page 154.

FLATTERS, COLONEL PAUL-XAVIER
1832–1881   France
1870(?): Sent to Algeria with the French Army.
1880: Commanded an expedition to explore and survey the Sahara northeast of the Ahaggar Mountains.
1881: Expedition almost completely wiped out in an attack by Tuareg tribesmen. Flatters killed.
See map on page 154.

FORSKAL, PETER
1736(?)–1763   Sweden
1761: Left Copenhagen for Arabia as botanist with Niebuhr's scientific expedition.
1762–1763: Arrived at Juddah. Traveled in northern Yemen and the Yemenite highlands. Made a separate expedition to gather herbs in the hills.
1763: Set out for Ṣan'ā'. At Ta'izz contracted fever. Died at Yarim.
1775: His *Flora Aegyptiaco-Arabica* published posthumously
See Niebuhr map on page 64.

FOUCAULD, FATHER CHARLES EUGÈNE DE
1858–1916   France
1881: Fought against the Algerian insurgents at Bu-Amama and traveled in Morocco.
1890: Entered a Trappist monastery.
1905: Built a hermitage at Tamanrasset in the Sahara. Lived a life divided between prayer and his studies of the

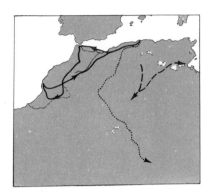

Tuareg tribesmen.
1916: Assassinated by hostile Tuaregs.

FOUREAU, FERNAND
dates unknown   France
1868–1898: From his home in Algeria,
made numerous journeys into the
Sahara, and grew to know the desert
well.
1898–1900: Led an expedition with a
military escort under Major Lamy
through the Sahara to the Sudan.
Continued to Lake Chad. At Kousserai,
defeated an army from Bornu. Proved
that a well-armed force could defy the
Tuareg and cross the desert.
See map on page 154.

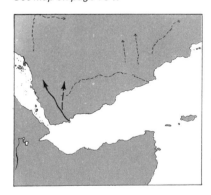

GLASER, EDWARD
1855–1908   Austria
1880–1890(?): Traveled to Marib,
sponsored by the French Académie des
Inscriptions et Belles Lettres. The
Himyaritic inscriptions he collected are
an important source of information
about pre-Islamic Arabia.

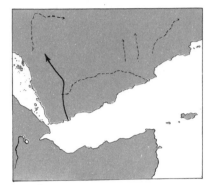

HALÉVY, JOSEPH
1827–1917   France
1869–1870: Visited Yemen. Examined
ruins of the Marib dam, visited ancient
cities and collected some 600
Himyaritic inscriptions. Visited the
Jewish colony at the oasis of Nejran.

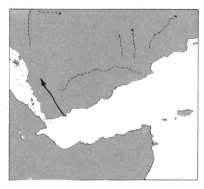

HARRIS, W. B.
1866–1933   England
1892: Traveled to Ṣan'ā' to see the
anti-Turkish revolt. Had a narrow
escape from ambush near the city.
Later published a number of books
about his travels.

HORNEMANN, FREDERICK KONRAD
1772–1801   Germany
1796: Presented his planned route to
the African Association for approval.
1797: Sailed from Marseille to Egypt.
1798–1799: Traveled, disguised as a
Moslem, with a caravan to Siwah and
Marzūq. Explored the district for seven
months.
1800: Crossed the Sahara with the
Bornu caravan, traveled to Katsina and
south toward the Niger River.
1801: Died at Bokani, a day's journey
from the Niger.
See map on page 123.

HOUGHTON, MAJOR DANIEL
1740(?)–1791   Ireland
1790–1791: Commissioned by the
African Association to find Timbuktu.
Set out east from the Gambia River.
Crossed the rivers Gambia and Senegal
and reached Simbing. Disappeared.
See map on page 123.

IBN-BATUTA (MOHAMMED IBN ABDULLA)
1304–1377(?)   Morocco
1325–1327: Made the pilgrimage to
Mecca, visiting Alexandria, Cairo, and
Upper Egypt. In Damascus, joined
pilgrim caravan for Mecca. Later visited
Baghdad and traveled extensively in
the Middle East.
1327–1330: Lived in Mecca.
1330–1332: Went to East Africa, on to
Ṣan'ā' and Aden. Sailed down the
coast of Africa, then followed the
Arabian coast from Dhofar to the
Persian Gulf.
1332–1349: Journeyed to central
Asia, India, and China.
1349–1353: Set out from Tangier for
Timbuktu. Reached as far south as Silla
on the Niger.
See maps on pages 64 and 123.

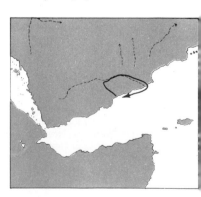

INGRAMS, WILLIAM HAROLD
born 1897   England

1934: Appointed resident adviser at
Al Mukallā. With his wife, Doreen,
tried to get to know and understand the
peoples of the Hadhramaut.
1937: Negotiated a treaty with the
Sultan of Shihr and Al Mukullā.
Negotiated the Ingrams truce between
the Hadhramaut tribesmen.
Traveled in the inland areas and
visited the Seiar Bedouins, who live
in the region bordering on the
Empty Quarter.
(?): With Doreen Ingrams, awarded
Royal Geographical Society gold
medal and Royal Asian Society bronze
medal for journals.

LAING, MAJOR ALEXANDER GORDON
1793–1826   Scotland
1822: Sent by governor of Sierra Leone
to open trade and prepare the way for
abolition of slavery in Kambian and
Mandingo countries. Became interested
in Niger exploration.
1825–1826: Left Tripoli to explore the
Niger. Crossed the Sahara to Timbuktu.
1826: Murdered by Arab tribesmen on
leaving Timbuktu.
See map on page 123.

LANDER, RICHARD LEMON
1804–1834   England
1825: With Clapperton, set out to reach
the Niger from Badagri.
1827–1828: On death of Clapperton,
returned to England and received
backing for an expedition in his own
right.
1830: With John Lander, traveled to
Bussa and sailed down the Niger to
the coast, finally establishing the
position of the river's mouth.
1832–1834: Led expedition up the
Niger. Fatally wounded by Africans.
See map on page 123.

LAPERRINE, GENERAL MARIE JOSEPH FRANCOIS HENRI
1860–1920   France
1901 (?)–1910: Commander in chief of
the Saharan Oases. Broke the power of
the Tuareg by forming camel corps of
desert tribesmen. Subdued the Sahara
to French control.
1920: Killed in an airplane crash on a

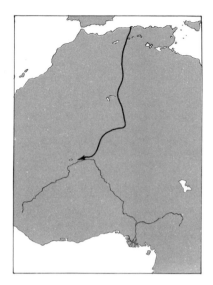

flight to establish an air route across the
Sahara.

LEDYARD, JOHN
1751–1789   United States
1776–1779: As corporal of marines
sailed in the *Resolution* with Captain
Cook on his last expedition.
1787: Reached St. Petersburg, having
walked from Hamburg. Deported by
Russian police.
1788: Commissioned by African
Association to cross the Sahara from
Egypt to Timbuktu.
1789: Died in Cairo while looking for a
caravan to join.

LENZ, OSCAR
1848–1925   Germany
1879–1880: Crossed the Sahara from
Morocco to Timbuktu. Turned west and
reached the coast at the mouth of the
Senegal River.
1885–1887: Set out from the mouth of
the Congo River, to cross Africa.
Followed the Congo's course to the
center of Africa. Visited Lake
Tanganyika and Lake Nyasa (now Lake
Malawi).
See map on page 154.

LYON, GEORGE FRANCIS
1795–1832   England
1818: With Ritchie and Belford,
commissioned to explore travel
prospects south of Fezzan and find out
more about the course of the Niger.
Expedition fell short of aims, but Lyon
reported on slave trade.

NACHTIGAL, GUSTAV
1834–1885   Germany
1869: Commissioned to deliver gifts
from King of Prussia to Sultan of
Bornu. Traveled to Fezzan, and explored
the Tibesti Massif.
1870–1874: Crossed the Sahara to
Lake Chad region, then continued to
Darfur and Kordofan. Reached Cairo
via the Nile Valley.
1882: Appointed German consul in
Tunis.
1884: As imperial commissioner visited
West Africa and annexed Togo and
Kamerun (Cameroon).
See map on page 154.

NIEBUHR, CARSTEN
1733–1815   Germany
1761: Left Copenhagen with six-man
scientific expedition sponsored by the
King of Denmark.
1762–1763: Arrived at Juddah.
Traveled in northern Yemen and the
Yemenite highlands. Explored the
Tihama.
1763: Left Al Mukhā for Ṣanʿāʾ, the
Yemenite capital. Stayed there 10 days,
then returned to Al Mukhā.
1764–1767: Niebuhr, now alone,
traveled in India, then returned to
Copenhagen via Muscat, the Persian
Gulf, Iraq, and Aleppo.
See map on page 64.

OVERWEG, ADOLF
1823–1852   Germany
1850–1852: Joined Richardson/Barth
expedition from Tripoli to Lake Chad
and the Niger. Before reaching Lake
Chad the three men separated and when
Overweg reached the lake he was very
ill. Explored Lake Chad but died before
starting for Timbuktu with Barth.
See map on page 123.

PALGRAVE, WILLIAM GIFFORD
1826–1888   England
1862: With a Syrian called Barakat,
crossed the An Nafūd desert. Reached

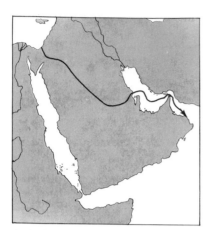

the Nejd and continued to Hofuf and Al
Qatif, becoming the first European to
cross the Arabian Peninsula from west
to east.

PARK, MUNGO
1771–1806   Scotland
1794: Commissioned by the African
Association to explore the Niger.
1795: Set out from the Gambia River
basin with two companions.
1796: Imprisoned by Moors for three
months. Escaped and continued alone
to the Niger. Discovered the river
flowed eastward.
1797: Returned to England.
1805: Sent to Africa to find the mouth
of the Niger. At Sansanding, built a
boat, and started down the river.
1806: Attacked by Africans at the falls
of Bussa and drowned while trying to
escape.
See map on page 123.

PHILBY, HARRY ST. JOHN
BRIDGER
1885–1960   England
1915: British agent in Iraq.
1917–1922: Traveled extensively in
Arabia and the Middle East.
1930: Converted to Islam. Adviser to
King Abdul Aziz ibn Saud of Saudi
Arabia.
1931: Trekked from Hofuf across the
Al Jāfūrah Desert then south to Shanna.
At Shanna turned west and crossed the
Empty Quarter to As Sulayyil.
1936: Traveled in southwest Arabia

between Mecca and Al Mukallā on the
Gulf of Aden.
See map on page 85.

PITTS, JOSEPH
1663–1731 (?)   England
1678: Captured by pirates off the north
coast of Africa. Sold into slavery.
1685: Made the pilgrimage to Mecca
with his master.
1704: Published the first authentic
account by an Englishman of the
pilgrimage to Mecca.

RICHARDSON, JAMES
(?)–1851   England
1845: Sent by British Bible Society to
investigate slave trade across the
Sahara. Traveled from Tripoli to the
oasis of Ghudāmis, then on to Ghāt.
1850: Led an expedition, accompanied
by Barth and Overweg, from Tripoli to
Lake Chad. Before reaching Lake
Chad the three men separated to
explore alone.
1851: Died of fever before reaching
Kukawa, where he was due to
rendezvous with Barth and Overweg.
See map on page 123.

RITCHIE, JOSEPH
(?)–1818   Scotland
1818: Led an expedition including
Lyon and Belford from Tripoli to
Fezzan. At Marzūq died from malaria.
See map on page 123.

ROHLFS, GERHARD
dates unknown   Germany
1862: Disguised as a religious official,
traveled in Morocco, visiting the oasis
of Tafilalt.
1863: Left Tafilalt for Timbuktu.
In Salah ran short of money, and turned
north for Ghudāmis and Tripoli.
1865: Crossed the Sahara from Tripoli
to Lagos, via Marzūq and Lake Chad.
1867–1881: Further travels in Africa.
See map on page 154.

SEETZEN, ULRICH JASPAR
1767–1811   Germany
1802–1805: Traveled via Vienna and
Constantinople to Asia Minor, Syria,
and Palestine.
1806: Visited Jordan and the Dead Sea.

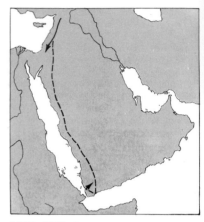

1807–1809: Spent two years in Egypt,
visiting the Pyramids, the Cataracts, and
the lake of Birkat Qārūn.
1809: Made the Pilgrimage to Mecca.
1810: Left Medina for Al Mukhā.
1811: Died, apparently from poison, in
the region of Ta'izz.

THESIGER, WILFRED PATRICK
born 1910   England
1930: Appointed honorary attaché to
the Duke of Gloucester's mission to
Ethiopia.
1934: Explored the Awāsh River in
Ethiopia.
1935–1939: In the Sudan Political
Service explored from Khartoum to the
Darfur mountain region and Tibesti
Massif.
1945: Joined a group working to
control the spread of locusts in the
desert. Became interested in the Empty
Quarter.
1945–1950: Traveled extensively in
southern Arabia. Twice crossed the
Empty Quarter.
See map on page 85.

THOMAS, BERTRAM SYDNEY
1892–1950   England
1920–1930: Political officer at Shatra
in Iraq. Served in Trans-jordan. Became
financial adviser to Sultan of Muscat
and Oman.
1926: Traveled from Gulf of Oman to
Ash Shāriqah on the Persian Gulf.
1928–1929: Traveled in the area
Dhofar.

1930: Set out from Dhofar to cross the
Empty Quarter (Rub' al Khali).
1931: Passed through Shanna and, the
crossing completed, reached the coast
at Doha on the Persian Gulf.
See map on page 85.

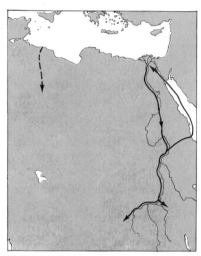

TINNE, ALEXANDRINE
1839–1869   Holland
1863–1864: Traveled from Khartoum
up the Bahr el Ghazal. Later traveled
in Algeria and Tunisia.
1869: Set out to cross the Sahara,
but was attacked and murdered by
Ahaggar tribesmen after leaving
Marzūq.

VARTHEMA, LUDOVICO DI
dates unknown   Italy
1502: Left Italy.
1503–1508: Visited Alexandria, Cairo,
and Damascus. Left Damascus with
the hajj caravan for Mecca.
1508–1510: Visited Juddah and
Yemen. Traveled widely in India and in
the East Indies.
See map on page 64.

VOGEL, EDWARD
1829–1856   Germany
1853: Sent to Lake Chad to find Barth
and Overweg.
1854: Reached Lake Chad, found
Barth, then continued alone to Zinder,
intending to explore the Lower Niger.

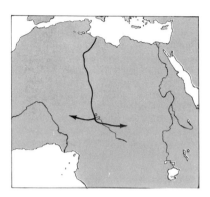

1856: Murdered by natives, when
traveling eastward toward the Nile.

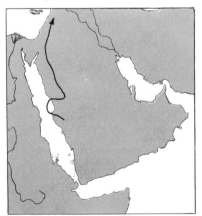

WAVELL, ARTHUR JOHN BYNG
(?)–1916   England
1891: Traveled to Ṣanʻā'.
1908–1909: Made the pilgrimage to
Mecca, traveling on the Hejaz Railway
for part of the journey.
1910: Attempted to explore south-
central Arabia.
1915(?): Raised force known as
Wavell's Own in East Africa.
1916: Killed in an ambush.

WELLSTED, LIEUTENANT JAMES
dates unknown   England
1834: Visited Husn Ghorab near Bi'r
'Alī in the Hadhramaut.
1834–1835: Explored in the region of
Muscat and Oman.
1835: From Belhaf, traveled to the ruins

of Nakab al Hajar, on one of the first
European expeditions to the interior of
southern Arabia.
See map on page 64.

Glossary

Arabs: Originally the Arabs were the nomads who inhabited the Arabian Peninsula. During the A.D. 600's and 700's these Semitic peoples, inspired by the teachings of Mohammed, overran the Middle East and northern Africa. Today, the term *Arab* is used to describe any person who uses the Arabic language in everyday conversation. Most Arabs are Moslems.

Arabic: one of the world's most widely used languages, Arabic is spoken by about 120 million people. It is a Semitic tongue and is related to Hebrew. The majority of the people throughout the Middle East and northern Africa speak Arabic. The people of the Arabian Peninsula were the first to use this language. Many English words come directly or indirectly from Arabic. Most of them begin with *al,* an Arabic word for *the—* albatross, alcohol, alfalfa, algebra.

Barbary pirates: Sea robbers from the Barbary States—present-day Morocco, Algeria, Tunisia, and Libya. Between about 1550 and the early 1800's these pirates roamed the Mediterranean Sea attacking and robbing the ships of other nations.

Bedouin: Any member of the nomadic Arab tribes who inhabit the desert areas of the Arabian Peninsula, Syria, Egypt, and North Africa. The name comes from the Arabic word *badawíy,* meaning desert dweller. Most Bedouins live by raising livestock—some own only camels, while others keep sheep and horses.

Berbers: Hamitic people living along the western coast of North Africa and also inland in the Sahara Desert. Most Berbers are Moslems and speak Arabic as well as Berber.
See also Tuareg

birka: A reservoir in the desert, usually built of stone, to provide water for travelers. One of the earliest birkas was built in the early 800's by order of Zubeidah, widow of Harun al-Raschid, the Caliph of Baghdad, for the use of pilgrims crossing the Nejd.

blood feud: A long-lasting mutual hostility between tribes, members of tribes, or families, involving continual killings in revenge for previous injuries or murders.

caliph: Historically, title of religious and civil leader of a Moslem state, e.g. Caliph of Baghdad. The caliph was usually elected, only two caliphates being hereditary. The caliph had to be an adult male, sound in mind and body. From the Arabic *khalifa* (a successor), the word designates a successor of Mohammed.

caravan: A group of merchants, pilgrims, or other travelers who journey together for the sake of security, in particular across the desert. The word also refers to the vehicles or pack animals used by such a group.

dervish: A Moslem friar who leads a life of poverty and self-denial. There are several orders of dervishes—one is known for the dancing and whirling which the dervishes perform as part of their worship, and which can induce ecstatic trances.

dhura: A cereal grass *(Sorghum vulgare)* which is grown in tropical and subtropical countries.

dysentery: A severe disease causing inflammation of the colon. It can be accompanied in serious cases by pain, fever, delirium, and bleeding. There are two kinds of dysentery: amebic (found mainly in warm and tropical countries); and bacillary (occurring in all climates, mostly in summer).

ergs: Area of sand dunes in the desert.

frankincense: A gum resin obtained from trees of the genus *Boswellia* found in Africa and Asia. A deep cut is made in the trunk of the tree and a small piece of bark removed. From this a milky juice exudes in drops. After two or three months' exposure to the atmosphere, the drops become hardened into *tears.* They are used as incense in religious services. Perfumers

obtain *essential oil,* an additive which gives perfume its long-lasting scent, from frankincense resin.

Hadhramaut: The Wadi Hadhramaut is a great fertile valley that passes through southwestern Arabia in the region of what are now Yemen and Saudi Arabia. It is some 300 miles long, with walls often 1,000 feet high. But the name Hadhramaut is also used loosely to describe the dry hilly plateau that separates the central desert from the narrow coastal plain in the south.

hajj: The pilgrimage to the holy city of Mecca which the Koran commands every adult Moslem to make at least once during his lifetime if he can afford it. Most Moslems who make the hajj also visit the Mosque of Mohammed at the holy city of Medina, more than 200 miles to the north of Mecca.

Hejaz: The western region of Arabia, consisting of a narrow coastal plain and, inland, a mountain chain. The Hejaz contains the holy cities of Islam— the goals of the Moslem pilgrimage. Mecca, one of the oldest cities of Arabia, is the birthplace of Mohammed, and Medina, to the north, the burial place of the prophet.

Himyarites: The ancient people who conquered Yemen in 115 B.C. and remained in control until A.D. 300. Scholars use the term Himyaritic to classify the language used by the Sabaean civilizations.
See also Sabaeans

ihram: The dress worn by Moslem pilgrims on the last stage of their journey to Mecca. It consists of two pieces of cotton cloth, one of which is wrapped around the waist, the other thrown over the left shoulder and knotted at the back.

Incense Trail: The ancient commercial route in Arabia. Goods were transported on the Incense Trail from southern Arabia, up through the Arabian Peninsula, and on to the Mediterranean Sea. Frankincense and myrrh were two of the most valuable substances carried by camel over the Incense Trail, but spices and silks from India and the East were also transported in this way. Great wealth was accumulated by the Arabs who produced and exported these precious goods and by those who transported them over the Incense Trail. Only after the 1500's, when the Portuguese opened new sea routes to the East, was trade diverted from the Incense Trail.

infidel: Generally, a heathen or unbeliever. Historically, Christians referred to Moslems as infidels, and vice versa.

Islam: The religion of the Moslems, founded by Mohammed in Arabia in the A.D. 600's. The basis of Islam is belief in the supreme majesty of the one true God — Allah. The first duty of a Moslem is unquestioning obedience to the will of Allah as interpreted by the Prophet Mohammed. The four main duties the Moslem must perform are prayer, fasting, alms-giving, and the pilgrimage to Mecca.

Kaaba: The sacred shrine in the Great Mosque at the holy city of Mecca. Every Moslem pilgrim who visits the city is required to make seven circuits of this holy building and to kiss the Black Stone which is built into a corner of the wall. The name comes from an Arabic word, *ka'ba,* meaning, literally, a square or cubical house.

kouskous: A North African dish of granulated flour steamed over broth. Its name comes from the Arabic word *kaskasa,* meaning to pound.

Koran: The sacred book of Islam. It contains the revelations made to Mohammed by the angel Gabriel. These revelations were written down by Mohammed's followers after his death. Moslems believe the Koran to be the word of God, and not simply the teachings of Mohammed.

Mamelukes: From the Arabic word *mamlūk,* meaning a slave. The Mamelukes originally arrived in Egypt as prisoners of war from Europe and Circassia (southern Russia). They were converted to Islam and, although they were at first slaves, they later became soldiers and served in the government. In A.D. 1250, they seized control of Egypt and ruled the country until the Turks conquered it in 1517.

Moors: Moslem peoples of mixed Arab/Berber stock who live in north-western Africa. The Moors invaded Spain in the 700's, and were only finally driven out in 1492.Today, the word *Moor* is used to describe all Moslem Arabic-speaking peoples of northwestern Africa. The name comes from the Latin word *Mauri,* which the Romans used to describe the peoples of this part of Africa.

Moslem: A follower of the Islam faith.

mosque: A Moslem temple or place of worship.

myrrh: A sweet-smelling, transparent gum resin obtained from the bark of trees of the genus *Commiphora,* which grow in eastern Africa and Arabia. Myrrh is used in the preparation of perfume and incense.

nomad: A member of a race or tribe that is continually moving from place to place in search of new pastures for its animals.

Sabaeans: A tribe of people who, in 950 B.C., invaded the mountains of Yemen and established their capital at Marib. Their kingdom was known as Saba and was possibly the kingdom of Sheba of the Bible. Scholars use the term Sabaeans to refer to the three kingdoms of Yemen which flourished between about 1400 B.C. and A.D. 300. *See also Himyarites*

sayid: The title given to a person who considers himself a descendant of Mohammed through his daughter Fatima. Until recently, sayids had supreme control over religion, law, and learning in the Hadhramaut.

sheik: An Arabic title referring either to an old and respected man or to the chief of a tribe or village. Sometimes a sheik is the leader of a religious society. Only Moslems use the title of sheik. The extent of a sheik's power usually depends upon his own will and character.

sultan: Title given to Moslem princes and rulers. The title has been used since about A.D. 900. The ruler of the Ottoman Empire was the greatest of the sultans. Today many sultans have wealth, but few have the power of the ancient princes.

Tuareg: The dominant group of nomadic Berber tribesmen who, until the present century, controlled much of the Sahara. The Tuareg have preserved their own language but many of them have become Moslems. The men wear veils, but, unlike other Moslems, the women go unveiled.

wadi: A river valley, where water only flows in the wet season. Wadis are found in northern Africa and Arabia, particularly in the Hadhramaut. There are often great stretches of fertile land in the wadis and in some towns have flourished for thousands of years.

Wahhabism: A reformation of Islam, which involved a return to the simple practices and teachings of Mohammed. Abd al-Wahhab first preached Wahhabism in the mid-1700's in the district of al-Ared in the southern Nejd.

Index

Picture Credits

Listed below are the sources of all the illustrations in this book. To identify the source of a particular illustration, first find the relevant page on the diagram opposite. The number in black in the appropriate position on that page refers to the credit as listed below.

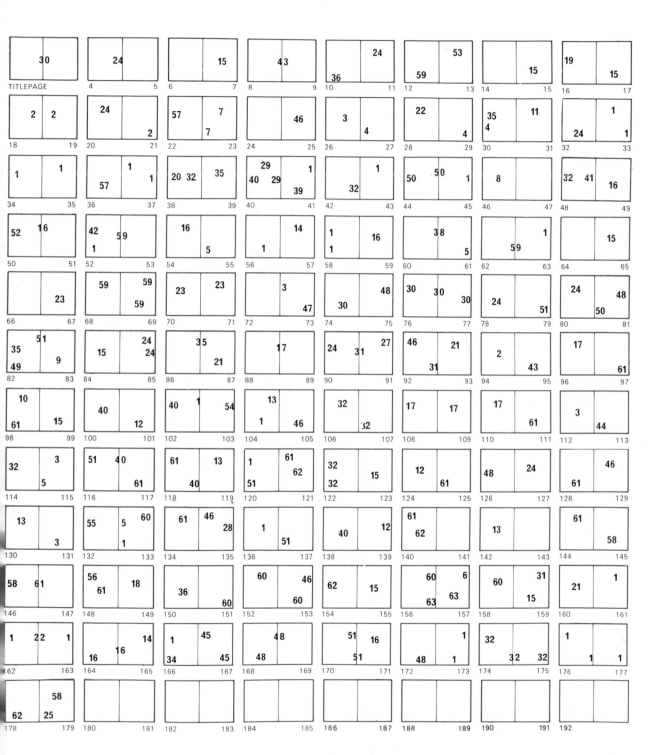